THINK
AND
GROW RICH

THE LEGACY

THINK
AND
GROW RICH

THE LEGACY

JAMES WHITTAKER

SOUND WISDOM

P.O. Box 310

Shippensburg, PA 17257-0310

For more information on publishing and distribution rights, call 717-530-2122 or info@soundwisdom.com.

Quantity Sales. Special discounts are available on quantity purchases by corporations, associations, and others. For details, contact the Sales Department at Sound Wisdom.

While efforts have been made to verify information contained in this publication, neither the author nor the publisher assumes any responsibility for errors, inaccuracies, or omissions.

While this publication is chock-full of useful, practical information, it is not intended to be legal or accounting advice. All readers are advised to seek competent lawyers and accountants to follow laws and regulations that may apply to specific situations.

The reader of this publication assumes responsibility for the use of the information. The author and publisher assume no responsibility or liability whatsoever on the behalf of the reader of this publication.

Interior design by Terry Clifton

ISBN 13 HC: 978-1-64095-018-4

ISBN 13 TP: 978-1-64095-019-1

ISBN 13 Ebook: 978-1-64095-020-7

For Worldwide Distribution, Printed in the U.S.A.

HC   2 3 4 5 / 22 21 20 19

TP   1 2 3 4 5 / 22 21 20 19

*To Napoleon Hill, whose teachings
transformed the world.*

*May your legacy continue to illuminate
the potential inside all of us.*

CONTENTS

FOREWORD

by Bob Proctor

IT WAS SATURDAY AFTERNOON, OCTOBER 21ST, 1961. Ray Stanford looked me right in the eye and said, "If you read some of this book every day and do exactly what it suggests, you can have anything you want."

I looked at him, I looked at the book, and realized he was not joking. Ray did not know me well, but he did know me well enough to know that I had virtually no formal education; a mere two months of high school. He was aware that I had no real business experience, and it was fairly obvious that I had a relatively poor attitude at best. I knew he knew that. Yet, he looked at me and said, "Read this. You can have anything you want." All I could think of was—*what's in that book?*

Ray spoke with such absolute conviction, I realized he was serious. The truth is, he made me want to read the book. So, I decided I would attempt to read a bit of it every day. I say attempt, because up to that point in my life I had never read a whole book. I was 26 years old, obviously lost, and going nowhere. This was my introduction to *Think and Grow Rich*.

Fortunately, I believed what Ray Stanford told me, and ever since that day so many years ago, I've attempted, to the best of my ability, to follow the advice that Napoleon Hill recorded for us in his classic book, *Think and Grow Rich*. Hill's book enabled me to build a company that operates all over the world. It's helped me earn millions of dollars. And, today, at 83 years of age, I'm still going as strong as I was when I was 26 and first picked up the book...well virtually as strong!

It's important for me to point out, I read *Think and Grow Rich* every day—*every* day. When I think of the book being Napoleon Hill's legacy, all that comes to my mind is: Wow, what a legacy!

James Whittaker has done a marvelous job in capturing Napoleon Hill's legacy. All the main points, the principles that Hill so clearly communicated are outlined in interesting stories; stories of people in situations where Hill's research was put to work.

As you go through this book, clearly understand that any one of the principles outlined in this book and properly incorporated into your personality will compound your effectiveness tenfold. I suggest that you make these principles a part of your way of thinking, a part of your way of life. Commit to it and watch your life change. I recall Ray saying to me, "If they did, you can." Although I didn't realize it at that moment, I believed in Ray's belief in me and that enabled me to move forward.

Study each of the principles in this book, relate to the stories and people, and realize as Napoleon Hill pointed out all those years ago, "There is one mind, one power that flows to and through every one of us." That power will do for you, what it's done for countless people worldwide.

Use the information in this book. Build your image. Strengthen your will. Give it everything you've got and expect, with every fiber of your being, the good that you desire. Napoleon Hill's legacy does live on, through me, though you, and now through this collection of inspiring stories in this wonderful book, *Think and Grow Rich: The Legacy.*

INTRODUCTION

THE Napoleon Hill journey has become the stuff of legend. At the turn of the 20th century, the young reporter was given a mission to interview some of the most successful people of his time. As Hill progressed, he quickly realized this pursuit would become his life's work. It led him to interview more than 500 of the world's most accomplished business leaders to unearth the secrets to their vast fortunes and identify whether any of their attributes could be modeled by everyday people. Hill met with industry titans such as inventor Thomas Edison, automobile giant Henry Ford, and steel magnate Andrew Carnegie—who, despite arriving in the United States a penniless immigrant, managed to accumulate one of the greatest personal fortunes in existence.

After more than 25 years of research on these extraordinary figures, Hill published his findings in *Think and Grow Rich*. The book outlined a success formula known as the "achievement philosophy" and was an instant phenomenon.

Perhaps Hill's greatest discovery was that those who succeed in any industry do so irrespective of their circumstances—that potential is not predicated on age, race, education, gender, or financial starting point. Those who consistently and purposefully apply the formula can achieve success beyond their wildest dreams.

Eighty years and more than 100 million copies later, *Think and Grow Rich* continues to inspire ordinary people to do extraordinary things. As the bestselling self-help book of all time, it has influenced people within every industry in the world and is the playbook that has enabled countless entrepreneurs, thought leaders, and cultural icons to rise above their circumstances.

Many of those interviewed for *Think and Grow Rich: The Legacy* noted that continual reading of Hill's timeless classic gave them profound insights at each step in their journey. When they experienced the power of applying the book's principles firsthand, their curiosity was sufficiently piqued to warrant not only repeat reading—in Bob Proctor's case, every day for 55 years—but also giving the book to inspire friends, colleagues, and loved ones. All the interviewees also noted that Hill's achievement philosophy is more relevant now than ever before.

Think and Grow Rich: The Legacy shares unflinchingly honest accounts from an eclectic group, aged from their twenties to their eighties, across dozens of industries. All these people found personal fulfillment in the unlikeliest (and in some cases, most tragic) of circumstances and have made their mark on the world. These stories aim to inspire and motivate you to action, while offering important pointers for you to map your own path to success.

Only you can define what "success" means for you, but ensure your definition is far broader than a big bank balance or Hollywood-level fame. For many, it is a holistic alignment of a healthy body, positive relationships, and the financial means to help not only themselves, but the people and causes they care about too—the ultimate freedom to live life on their own terms. As you will see from the accounts in this book, while some enjoy a more public forum for their achievements, just as many find their deepest fulfillment behind closed doors.

Today, success is easier to achieve than ever before, but you must recognize that poverty consciousness automatically occupies the mind that is not success conscious. To stay focused, turn up the volume on your inner voice. With the right roadmap, there is no distraction strong enough to knock you off the path to self-mastery.

Prosperity flows to those who build a plan and take consistent, purposeful action to get there. Before you start the first chapter, think about what you want from your life—*your* life. With a clear picture in mind, you can readily apply each principle and advance with purpose.

This book is released in conjunction with the film *Think and Grow Rich: The Legacy* to offer an updated delivery of the greatest self-help book of all time and to inspire today's generations to success. The ultimate tribute to Napoleon Hill and *Think and Grow Rich* is the inspirational stories of those who have used his achievement philosophy to change their lives for the better. As you turn the pages, you too may be struck with an idea that will change the world forever.

Everything you need to create a truly rich life is already in your possession, and this book shows you how to make it happen.

Welcome to *Think and Grow Rich: The Legacy.*

DESIRE

THE STARTING POINT OF ALL ACHIEVEMENT

"There is one quality which one must possess to win, and that is definiteness of purpose, the knowledge of what one wants, and a burning desire to possess it."
—NAPOLEON HILL

DESIRE, THE STARTING POINT OF ALL ACHIEVEMENT, is the necessary kindling for anyone wishing to achieve extraordinary success. Prosperity does not flow to those indifferent toward their destination. A small, weak flame is extinguishable by the slightest breeze, yet the same flame, if properly stoked, can be transformed into a great blaze.

And still so many of us are half-hearted about our deepest desires. The most outstanding revelation of our time—*that human beings can change their lives by changing their thoughts*—requires that someone possess a burning desire directed toward a definite purpose. This desire must be strong—to the point of obsession—until the goal is achieved or the object is attained. Understand also that desire must be directed at both thought and the daily actions necessary to make your dream a reality.

We all have within us right now everything we need to succeed—this will become more and more evident as you read this book. If we harness our abilities and direct them toward this definite purpose, we will be rewarded bountifully. However, if we give in to idleness and allow indifference to become our dominating attribute, we will reap the poor crop that we have sown, manifested in poverty, illness, and misery.

Pay careful attention to your state of mind because it will act on whatever it is you focus on most. Those with negative thoughts should offer no complaint when negative circumstances enter their life, just as those who nurture positive thoughts should offer no apologies when they are blessed with good fortune.

Today, we are the most advanced and connected society in history, but with it comes great distraction. Do not be swayed by the hollow, the deceptive, or the farcical. Instead, turn up the volume on your inner voice. Then, stand by your dream until it becomes a physical reality. Desire is the first of Hill's principles, but to be effective it must be pursued with unrelenting action and the persistence to see it through to the end.

Why is it that so many people accept whatever life hands them rather than taking the time to conjure their wildest dreams, create a plan for their attainment, and then work toward that definite aim each day? With each page you turn, remember that the state of mind necessary for the highest assurance of success is desire to the point of obsession.

Janine Shepherd

Janine Shepherd felt the burn in her legs as she powered round another turn in the rugged Blue Mountains, just outside Sydney. Her legs trembled, and her chest heaved, but her desire for victory was unparalleled. Behind her, a small swarm of cyclists had got used to seeing Shepherd's outline in front of them: every time they drew close, she would summon more strength to stay ahead of the pack.

Shepherd loved the hill climbs, and her goal for the ride was to lead all the way to the top. In the last half-hour of the six-hour climb, every turn of the pedal hurt as the lactic acid grew. But unlike most people, each wince of pain fueled her determination. To Shepherd, pain meant progress. That progress would chip away at a particularly lofty goal—to become the first athlete in Australia's history to win Gold at the Winter Olympics—which she hoped to achieve later that year in Calgary.

Her teeth clenched, she powered on. Possessed with her goal, the 24-year-old—nicknamed "Janine the Machine" for her tenacious spirit and competitive fire—had no idea that the fight of her life, away from the ski fields and bike rides, drew close.

The driver of the sports utility had his mind else-where, as his speeding vehicle careened into one of the world's most promising athletes. In an instant, the earthy green landscape, wild eucalyptus fragrance, and sweeping views of the iconic countryside disappeared. With a bone-crunching thud, Shepherd's whole world went black.

~\ı/~

For 10 days, Janine Shepherd clung to life. Remarkably, even as her battered body lay limp and comatose, she felt awareness. It was a spiritual period unlike anything she'd ever known. "When I was in the physical dimension, I was aware of excruciating pain," she remembers, "while in the spiritual, I was detached from earthly concerns and pain-free." As a team of doctors scrambled to save her—beginning with the uncontrolled blood flow—waiting family and friends were told to expect the worst. The odds of even making it to the hospital alive had been slim, at best, given the magnitude of the accident and the severity of her injuries. But on arrival, a flicker of the eyes showed that Shepherd was conscious. With her condition still critical, the doctors devised a plan to give her some semblance of a body to return to.

While they plotted, Shepherd lay in intensive care at Sydney's Prince Henry Hospital, fighting the incredible pain that ravaged her battered frame. She had a broken neck, six broken vertebrae, five broken ribs, a broken collarbone, and multiple breaks to her right arm and feet. The force of the impact meant her scalp had to be stitched back to the skull, and a massive hematoma dominated her lower back and buttocks. She had also lost almost all of her own blood and was paralyzed from the waist down. Finally, there were extensive lacerations to her abdomen and right leg, which were still filled with gravel. Janine the Machine, who once recorded the highest VO2 max of any female athlete in Australian history, would need every bit of grit and determination to defy medical opinion and survive.

The days wore on, and her condition stabilized. As her body fought to heal what it could, Shepherd lay on a thin, firm bed to help stabilize her spine, while dozens of tubes and sensors monitored her condition, a morphine drip attempted to assist with pain relief, and a brace restricted her head movement. The boredom and frustration of hospital life was broken up by regular visits from a procession of medical professionals, including neurosurgeons, orthopedic physicians and rehabilitation specialists. Shepherd was eventually transferred to the acute spinal ward, to a room she shared with five other people. They enjoyed conversing with each other despite rarely being able to actually see each other, due to injury-related mobility issues. Sharing a room at such a raw time led to moments of authenticity, richness and connection that none of the patients had experienced previously. But when the conversation ceased, all Shepherd could do was stare at the world via the small mirror suspended above her bed, and pray for the nightmare to end.

Instead, one day while her parents were visiting, one of the doctors made an unscheduled visit to Shepherd's bedside with the unfortunate results of her myelogram. The scan revealed a burst fracture in her back, where an assortment of bony fragments were compressing her spinal cord. She would need surgery, as soon as they could arrange it, to decompress the spine and remove the bone fragments, while fusing a bone graft to make the spinal column rigid again. The risks were enormous for such a complex procedure in such a delicate part of the body, but it was necessary if she wanted any quality of life. Without the surgery, she would never walk again. With it, there was a glimmer of hope that she might.

It was not until later, as Shepherd processed the conversation between Dr. Blum and her parents, that the significance of her condition suddenly hit. Until that point, the professional skier had held hopes that once out of the hospital bed she would be back to her usual athletic self, possibly even making it to the Calgary Winter Olympics later that year as planned. But not being able to walk or ski again? Sports was not just her identity—it was *everything*. Not only was the nightmare not ending, it was getting worse. Overwhelmed as the dire situation sank in, Shepherd screamed, "Please, someone help me!" A nurse rushed to her aid. Lying on the stiff bed, Shepherd wept. In between sobs, she begged for answers—"Why me? Why has this happened?"—as the sedative gradually took effect.

After the spinal surgery, for 12 long weeks Australia's best skier lay helpless and immobilized, without knowing if it had been a success. Then, the prognosis. "The operation went as well as we could have hoped, and we've picked as much bone out of your spinal cord as we could," the doctors explained. "But the damage is permanent. You're what we call a partial paraplegic—you have no feeling from the waist down, and at most you might get 10–20% return. You'll have to use a catheter for the rest of your life, and if by some miracle, you are able to walk again, it will be with calipers and a walking frame. You'll need to rethink everything in your life."

Six months later, as her father wheeled her out of hospital, Shepherd felt the sun on her face for the first time since the accident. Never had she been so grateful for a simple ray of sunlight. But there was still adjustment to be made. Returning home, frequent waves of depression scuttled any plans she had of returning to normality. "I wanted to run out the door and get my old life, and my old body, back," she recalls. Her weight had plummeted to 80 pounds, and even simple tasks she used to take for granted had become a mission. Fighting an exhausting mental battle while trying to make sense of what happened to her physical being, Shepherd struggled to cope. "I've lost everything," she exclaimed to her mom. "Why me?"

One particularly difficult day, she pushed herself to the edge of the bed, and fell to the floor. Wiping the tears from her eyes, she clasped her hands together and prayed to whoever might be listening. "Please God," she begged, "show me a way through or show me a way out."

Shepherd wondered about her friends from the spinal ward, some of who were *still* in the hospital. Maria, a girl who Shepherd had got close to, had been in a car accident and woke on her 16th birthday to the news that she was a quadriplegic—no movement from the head down. The teenager was always happy, always smiling, and never once complained. Reflecting on the whole situation, the national ski champion realized it was not *her* life, but life itself. It wasn't *her* pain; it was everybody's pain. And that left her with a simple choice—keep striving for gold in whatever life threw her way, or accept it and stop complaining. "Maria gave me the most precious gift in life: the gift of acceptance," Shepherd recounts.

With a sliver of tenacity emerging through the ashes, Janine the Machine reframed her situation. "Why *not* me?" she asked. "Maybe being at rock bottom is the perfect place to start."

⁓↘↙⁓

"I'm here for a flying lesson!" the woman said enthusiastically. The attendant stared at the plaster body cast, and the brittle frame she'd propped against the counter to hold herself up. "O-kay," he stammered, waving for assistance. "Can you walk?"

"No," Shepherd replied defiantly, "but I figured that if I can't walk, I'll fly." Minutes later, Janine Shepherd was driven out to the tarmac of the Bankstown Airport, lifted into the cockpit, and seated alongside her instructor, Andrew.

"Would you like to have a go at taxiing?" the instructor asked. "Just use your feet to control the pedals."

"I can't use my legs," Shepherd replied. "But I can use my hands."

As the engine rumbled, the low-wing Socata Tobago plane—in its distinct red, white and blue paint—careened along the tarmac and took off into the clear, blue sky, with the picturesque Sydney skyline in the background. It was a spectacular day. Pointing to the mountains in the distance, the instructor asked Shepherd to take the joystick and aim for one of the peaks. "As I grabbed the controls, I felt a million miles from the spinal ward," Shepherd recalls. "I knew right then I was going to be a pilot." As the plane soared over the countryside, the 24-year-old realized their target was the Blue Mountains—where her extraordinary journey had begun.

Elated by her first flight, she found the motivation to accelerate her rehabilitation and, as with her athletic career, she started recording her daily progress in a training log. "On my down days," she says, "I would look back through the log to remind myself of the progress I had already made." Shepherd set challenging goals, and each accomplishment spurred her on. In between corrective surgeries and rehabilitation, she would study everything she could on aviation. Finally, against the toughest of odds, Shepherd passed her pilot medical exam and was cleared to fly, eventually receiving her pilot's license. "The enormous sense of achievement was far greater than anything I had felt before—far more than winning a ski race, better than a triathlon podium finish, surpassing even the prospect of being an Olympic contender," she would later write of the thrill. "It wasn't part of the original plan, but that moment was my equivalent of an Olympic Gold Medal."

Excited with her new purpose, Shepherd continued expanding her aviation skills and qualifications. Eighteen months after leaving the spinal ward, Janine Shepherd returned to flight school as an instructor, teaching others how to fly.

⁓

Today, the woman who was given minimal hope of even living travels the world as a motivational speaker, sharing her incredible story with its core message of hope: that a broken body is not a broken person, reminding people that at any moment a single decision can change your life. The woman who was told she would never walk or have children is now able to move around unaided and is a proud mother to three children, while still being classified as a partial paraplegic. Eight years after the accident, and against medical advice, she was able to cross-country ski again.

"I just don't listen when people tell me I can't do something," she says firmly. Shepherd's love of flying led to her gaining a commercial pilot's license and becoming a trained aerobatics flying instructor, despite not having any feeling in her feet, as well as being the first female director of the Civil Aviation Safety Authority.

Among her extraordinary list of accomplishments, Shepherd has also authored five books, completed her college degree, been a torchbearer at the 2000 Paralympics, and has been awarded her country's highest civilian honor—the Order of Australia—for her service to the community, her inspiration and her work in raising awareness of spinal cord research. Her TEDx talk "A Broken Body Isn't a Broken Person" has been viewed millions of times.

In the digital age, where society is becoming increasingly concerned with image, Janine Shepherd shares her message that spirit far outweighs any physical representation: "Of one thing I'm certain: I am not my body, and you are not yours."

Grant Cardone

In Lake Charles, Louisiana, Grant and Gary Cardone skipped their way to the grocery store, grinning from ear to ear. The twins each had a quarter from their father, Curtis, to spend on whatever they wanted, and a quarter could buy a lot of bubblegum. Grant couldn't take his hands off the silver coin—he fiddled constantly with it as they scampered down the street. Alas, with one misstep, the quarter went flying out of his grasp and through the grate of a nearby manhole. The eight-year-old strained his little arms as far as he could, but the quarter was lost forever.

In tears, Grant ran home to tell his father what happened. "Never play with money," Curtis responded angrily. "Learn a good lesson. NEVER play with money!" Later that day, his grandfather, Tony, pulled him aside for more advice. "The trick is to make sure you never go anywhere with just one quarter," he said.

Eighteen months later, Curtis Cardone finally succumbed to the heart condition that had bothered him for years, and passed away aged 52. "From that day, we were forced to learn about money," Grant Cardone reflects. "But, worse, there was nothing we could do to get him back." Curtis' death was a huge blow to the family, and Grant's mother, Concetta, struggled with the responsibility of being the primary breadwinner and caregiver to their five children. Concetta had been left with a little money, but was not equipped with the skills to obtain more, so she tightened her belt and conserved the family's funds as best she could.

Not long after, Tony passed, and Grant battled with the loss of both male figureheads in his family. Whenever he complained about their situation, Concetta pleaded with him to be grateful for what they did have rather than resentful about what they lacked. Grant had no idea how he could help his mom get through the difficult period: "I was 10 years old. My uncle kept saying, 'Take care of your mom,' but I couldn't. My older brother kept saying, 'Grow up.' My sisters were telling me, 'Quit crying.' And I was waiting for a man to come in and show me what I could do, how I could make it all better." Despite his mother's best efforts to instill gratitude, Grant was frustrated with his loss and that everything was scarce. He grew up in America's middle-class, but hated every minute of it.

Entering his teenage years, Grant Cardone became even angrier—school was boring, the rest of the family bugged him, and his self-esteem continued to plummet. When his older brother died, all bets were off. At 15, someone introduced Cardone to drugs. "I knew it was wrong," he reflects, "but I hated myself." For the next 10 years he would use drugs every day.

He enrolled in college, because he thought it was what middle-class kids do. With vague aspirations of getting rich one day, but without a plan to make it happen, Cardone opted to study accounting. However, his boredom and resentment with study—with life—continued, and so did his cycle of self-destruction. He hung out with the wrong crowd, constantly abused alcohol, and indiscriminately consumed whatever drugs he could get his hands on: "Terminally hopeless," he describes his life at the time. Against the odds, Cardone graduated from college with an accounting degree he had no intention of using, but the relationship with his family was becoming increasingly strained, and he was now lumped with $40,000 in student loan debt. "Worse yet," he reflects, "I had no abilities, no self-esteem, and no direction."

His drug abuse continued, and he maintained a job at a car dealership to help fund his destructive lifestyle. Just as teenage Cardone had tried and failed to take care of his mother after his father's passing, so too did Concetta try to take care of her son in his time of need, and fall short. She did all she could to prevent his toxic choices from turning fatal, but eight years of constant drug abuse and its associated behavior tested even a mother's patience. On one occasion Cardone was beaten to within an inch of his life, arriving at hospital in an unrecognizable state and requiring 76 stitches in his head and face. Even this did little to put the brakes on the 23-year-old's downward spiral.

Finally, two years after the hospital visit and after a decade of distress, Cardone's souring relationship with his family reached a tipping point. "Enough!" Concetta exclaimed. "You're not welcome in my home. Don't come here anymore." Officially hitting rock bottom, Cardone checked into rehab.

Remarkably, despite his transgressions, he had managed to maintain the job at the car dealership, and his employer's insurance covered a 28-day stint in a treatment center for substance abuse. It was there that he was first able to string two days of sobriety together, then four days, then six days. While his time at the treatment center was not without incident, it helped the 25-year-old to understand that he didn't *have* to use drugs. After three weeks, as his mood started to stabilize, the staff told him he would need to continue taking a different drug—phenobarbital, a class-four narcotic—to help him maintain his new life as a recovering addict. This was a direct clash with Cardone's beliefs; he had resurrected his adolescent goals to write books, own a private jet, and be successful. "You cannot have any ideas of grandiosity," the staff advised him. "You need to give all that up, or you're going to go back to using drugs."

Further, the stint in rehabilitation had helped him realize that the only reason he took drugs in the first place was because he was a bored and angry 15-year-old with low self-esteem—it had simply been a detour, albeit a prolonged one. Confident that he would recover if he could control the variables that led to the cause in the first place, he felt that labeling him a lifetime drug addict—someone with an incurable disease—was unfair and counterproductive. "If I make a wrong turn on a road, that doesn't mean I can't turn around and go back," Cardone justified his attitude. The treatment center staff disagreed, and forecast his impending demise. "You'll never make it," they said. But Grant Cardone didn't need their opinions. Twenty-eight days clean and sober for the first time in 10 years, he had faith that if he could fall that low, he could climb just as high.

Believing that the answers lay within him, rather than in a pill bottle, his first order of business was to throw out every phenobarbital tablet. Then he took every ounce of his addictive, compulsive and obsessive qualities, and directed them at a frenetic pace toward making himself a success. Cardone ditched the no-hopers from his old life, and committed to cultivating a network of winners around him.

Luckily, his old job at the car dealership was waiting—especially fortunate since no one else would hire him. Cardone buried himself in work, but grew frustrated at his weak sales pipeline and paltry commissions. "Man, I *hate* this game," he vented. One colleague, Ray, reframed the situation for him. "The only reason you hate sales," Ray said, "is because you're no good at it. I've got something that might help." Ray lent him a cassette by a renowned sales trainer that contained a step-by-step playbook, from the moment you met a customer to when the sale was closed. Cardone was instantly hooked. He phoned the company to inquire about what other programs they offered, eventually investing $3,000 in a training program on 12 videotapes.

Regardless of what else was happening in his life, he committed an hour every day to watching and practicing the sales training techniques from the video program. Within 30 days, his sales pipeline doubled. "I'm actually starting to enjoy the sales game," Cardone bragged to Ray, more determined than ever. Within nine months, he was ranked in the top 1% of sales people within his industry. He had transmuted his biggest hurdle into his biggest strength. Better yet, he had identified a significant passion and went forth with a single purpose—to master the art of selling.

At 29 years of age, Cardone felt that the working environment at the car dealership had become toxic, and opted to test his skills on the open market with his own business. The day after quitting, he started an ambitious travel schedule around the country teaching high-end car dealers how to sell. He created a list of target businesses, then approached each one in person with a single line: "Hi, my name's Grant Cardone and I need three minutes of your time." In those three minutes, he would offer a brief demonstration of his sales tactics, showing how his services would translate to enormous revenue gain—underpinned with integrity—to revive the industry's reputation. "It's the hardest thing I've ever had to do," Cardone says of his door-knocking days. "If you can do that, you can do anything." Finally, he would conclude the appointment by asking for a check that would enable the company to send their people to an event Cardone was hosting. As his conversions increased, his asking rate went up.

His sales expertise, coupled with a ferocious work ethic, led to a quickly growing client base, all from a simple formula: find a high value audience, develop a product or service they are interested in, and demonstrate value. Cardone went through all his savings while he focused on making his new venture a success, relying on his own instincts rather than obtaining a business loan. He would visit up to 40 companies each day, frequently in cities where he didn't know a single person. Finally, after three years, the income justified his decision: his new business was a success. In place of substance abuse, Cardone had become addicted to learning how to sell, promote and market, all hallmark responsibilities of an entrepreneur. For the next few years, he hosted more than 200 workshops each year, and his reputation in sales began to grow.

To keep forward-focused, he would write his wildest dreams in a notebook he carried with him everywhere, with one catch—they were set in the present, as if they had already happened. Making a conscious decision to get into the property game, he wrote, "I own 20+ apartments" before he owned a single one. Soon after, on a business trip to La Jolla, California, the 35-year-old stood on the beach admiring the shoreline and came up with a new dream for his notebook: "I live in La Jolla, California, on the ocean," he wrote. Two years later, he had purchased his dream home within 50 feet of where he stood that day. Several years later, he would be the proud owner of more than 500 apartments throughout California.

By most metrics, Cardone was living the dream, but the sales expert still felt something was missing—he felt lonely. Turning again to his notebook, he wrote that he wanted to have a beautiful wife and two children. One day, he met his dream woman, Elena, in Los Angeles, but it took a year before she consented to go out with him. Another year later, they were husband and wife. "Elena has been a tremendous partner," Cardone says. "I truly wish that other people are able to end up with someone so supportive."

Today, Grant Cardone never travels anywhere with just one quarter. He is the CEO of five privately held companies with annual revenues of more than $100 million. He also presides over one of the largest private property empires in the US, owning more than 4,000 apartments generating millions in income each year. He is the author of seven bestselling books, runs educational programs through his Cardone University, and is in high demand throughout the world as a motivational speaker.

But his legacy is encouraging people to think much grander than their circumstances and, more importantly, in understanding what they're prepared to give up to get there. "Think and grow to where you want to be," is what Cardone believes. "I've been doing that every day since I was 25." Known for thinking big, the property mogul's mission is to positively impact the lives of seven billion people—almost every person on Earth.

He now lives in Miami, Florida, with Elena and their two children, with a shared purpose that keeps them moving in the same direction together. Cardone, true to his word, hasn't touched a single recreational drug in 34 years, relying on the power of the mind and a burning desire to succeed.

FAITH
VISUALIZATION OF, AND BELIEF IN, ATTAINMENT OF DESIRE

"Faith is the only known antidote to failure."
—NAPOLEON HILL

YOUR LEVEL OF SUCCESS DEPENDS ON THE THOUGHTS that enter your mind and what you do with them. Knowing that desire can be converted into its physical equivalent, the principle of faith—absolute certainty that you will achieve your goal—is used to remove limitations, allowing you to progress beyond temporary adversity that can often seem fatal.

Most people's ability to practice faith is diminished by their lack of self-confidence; however, it can be rebuilt through constant care and attention. One of the most powerful ways to do this is to continually write, memorize, and repeat positive affirmations. Once mastered, faith becomes the strongest and most productive of our emotions. Unmastered, it is like watching a still kettle on a cold stovetop and wondering why it doesn't boil.

Both poverty and wealth are the offspring of thought. Therefore, your most important duty is to protect your dreams by surrounding yourself with thoughts and people worthy of your definite purpose. It is equally important to keep yourself insulated from the people who flout your intentions, or the forked tongues that erode your spirit. Negative people slowly chew away at your ambitions like rats. But being wary of their involvement also means not stooping to their level and responding in kind. Negative attitudes can never bring a positive outcome, so significant focus should be placed on eliminating that from your own character first. As your positive mental attitude develops, others will begin to appreciate your belief in them and offer their unconditional support to you.

On working toward your definite purpose, place great emphasis on confidently repeating your intention out loud, allowing yourself to feel the object of your desire already within your possession. This process serves to train your subconscious to understand that whatever obstacle you face along the way, you have sufficient faith to see it through. Only through this repetitive practice will you convince your subconscious that the attainment of your desire is inevitable.

A lack of faith leads to fear, a dangerous emotion that causes poor decisions and irrational actions. At worst, it creates the habit of quitting, which is the surest way to prolonged failure. As you read on, you will see that it is the collaboration of the resources directed at your definite purpose, with unwavering faith in its eventual attainment, that brings success.

Jim Stovall

"Jim, we're not sure why, and we're not sure when, but we do know someday you'll be totally blind. And there's not one thing we can do about it."

Jim Stovall looked from one doctor's face to another's. All three specialists nodded gravely. Stovall's heart sank. That day, the 17-year-old was told to come to terms with a harsh reality—the life he loved would change forever.

As a youngster, Stovall had shown promise in several sports, but he held dreams of playing offensive tackle for the illustrious Dallas Cowboys. Standing six foot four inches tall and weighing 260 pounds, he thought he fulfilled all the physical requirements.

But during a routine physical for high school football, an anomaly was identified. Not only was he declared unfit to play, but he spent 11 months in and out of doctors' offices and hospitals undergoing tests to figure out what was wrong.

The doctors explained that Stovall's eyesight simply wasn't sharp enough for the sports he loved. His first response was to enter a state of extreme denial, pretending he had never received the news. But soon enough, as the doctors predicted, his vision began to fade.

For as long as he could remember, Stovall had attended church every week with his family. One Sunday he woke up frustrated and despairing. Kneeling by his bed, he took a deep breath, closed his eyes, and delivered a message: "God, if you're really out there, offer me a sign by the end of today that I have something to live for." He paused, allowing a moment for his request to transmit properly.

The state fair, a popular community event, was held later that day in his hometown of Tulsa, Oklahoma. Stovall went along and witnessed an exhibition from Olympic Games athletes across various fields, including gymnastics, running, and weightlifting. The gymnasts and runners he admired, but the third—weightlifting—was something he felt, given his physique, might be worth attempting. It gave Stovall a glimmer of hope that perhaps his athletic career had not expired after all.

He left the exhibition hall and strolled down to the arena, where he noticed a large sign for a free concert. Stovall walked to the front of the empty arena and sat in the first row. He thought about being blind, prayed some more, and wept as he considered what a lonely life he would lead. Meanwhile, behind him, the arena had started to fill. Finally, a voice boomed: "Ladies and gentlemen, please welcome to the stage Ray Charles!" The acclaimed blind musician stood just 12 feet in front of his seat. Watching someone with comparable vision impairments wowing audiences gave Stovall greater hope that there might be some life left inside him.

With a renewed sense of optimism, he opted to attend college after he graduated high school. One day he noticed a school for blind children across the road and, on a whim, walked in and asked if he could help out as a teacher. The attendant responded, "If you're serious, we have a kid you can work with one on one. You can either work with him or get out of here."

"What should I teach him?" Stovall asked.

"This kid, Christopher, is four years old. He's totally blind and has a lot of other physical problems. He'll never learn, grow, or develop any more than he already has. What we want you to do is keep him quiet and hidden away so as not to distract the other kids."

The attendant also offered two tips: first, to keep the boy's shoes tied so he wouldn't trip and hurt himself; and second, to keep him away from the stairs.

The first day, Stovall noticed Christopher was decidedly smaller than other kids his age, and this motivated Stovall to help even more. "Young man, before I leave here—no matter how many days, weeks, or months it takes—you're at least going to learn to tie your shoes and climb those stairs," he said.

"No, I can't," Christopher replied.

"Yes, you can."

The exchange continued, with both holding firm.

Each afternoon after his classes, Stovall would visit the school for the blind and help Christopher learn to tie his shoes and climb the stairs.

Several months later, the day he feared most arrived. Stovall woke up to find his vision had deteriorated significantly overnight. Even getting around by himself became extraordinarily difficult, and he could barely discern the words in his textbooks.

Stovall cautiously wandered over to the school for the blind and told them it would be his last day. "I'm going to have to drop out of college, and I can't volunteer anymore," he said. "I just can't make it."

Stovall had not realized that Christopher had been dropped off earlier than usual that day and was sitting outside the office. He could hear the entire conversation.

Stovall turned and saw the boy, told him he was leaving, and wished him well for the future. "I'm going to have to drop out of college, and I can't volunteer anymore," he said again. "I just can't make it."

"Yes, you can," Christopher said.

"No, I can't," Stovall replied.

"Yes, you can."

"No, I can't."

Finally, Stovall attempted to explain why his situation was different—except that with each word he began to feel like a fraud for refusing to take the advice he had offered Christopher for months. He thought to himself,

"Either quit lying to this kid or get up and do something with your life."

Then, as he thought about their respective situations, Stovall reasoned, "You know what? You're right. Whether in life or in business, there are some things worthy of your best effort, even small tasks like tying your shoes, walking upstairs, or attending college." He looked at Christopher and said, "You keep up your hard work and I promise to be here with you each day to help."

Three years later, Stovall graduated from college with two degrees—psychology and sociology—with honors. That week, with what little vision he had left, he saw Christopher climb three flights of stairs, sit on the final step, and tie both of his shoes. It was one of the last things he ever saw and one of the most profound lessons he ever learned. Wiping the tears from his eyes, Jim Stovall realized: "No matter what the dream inside you is, the answer is always 'Yes, you can.'"

His college friends had all received job offers from the corporate outreach events on campus; however, Stovall had not found any companies willing to hire an aspiring weightlifter destined for blindness. He returned home and told his father he would explore opportunities to start his own business—if no one else would employ him, he would start a company and employ himself. "Come back tomorrow and I'll give you something," his father replied. While they were far from being a wealthy family, Stovall thought his father might contribute financially to help him get the new venture off the ground.

They met as planned, and his father sat him down. "I'm actually going to give you two things," he started. "First, I'm going to give you the certain knowledge that if you ever get anything out of this life, you earned it on your own, because I'm not going to give you a dime."

"Okay, what's the second thing?" Stovall replied, hoping for something a little more tangible.

"If you want to be in business for yourself, I can't help you because I've never done that. But I know one very successful man, quite elderly, who has kindly agreed to mentor you. His name is Lee Braxton," his father said.

Stovall went to the old man's house, where he learned that, despite only having a sixth-grade education, Braxton was able to make $10 million during the Great Depression—the largest economic downturn in world history—and had since given almost this entire fortune away.

Braxton asked, "Can you read?"

"Yes, but it's very difficult."

"Good," Braxton replied as he pushed a copy of *Think and Grow Rich* into Stovall's hand. "Read it and come back when you're finished."

Stovall returned one week later, and Braxton tested his knowledge.

"Not good enough. Come back next week when you've actually understood it."

Next week, Stovall returned to Braxton's house and was able to demonstrate his knowledge of the book. They continued to meet frequently, using the principles of Hill's book as the framework for their conversations. It was much later that Stovall found out his mentor had been Napoleon Hill's best friend and delivered the eulogy at his funeral.

Their meetings helped Stovall understand that, while he would certainly go blind, the only thing over which he had true power were his thoughts. If he could control his thoughts, he could lead any life he chose.

They also spoke about one particular phrase at length: *Every failure brings with it the seed of an equivalent advantage.*

"Having my eyes completely fail must mean I have a very big advantage at something," he told his mentor.

"You're right," Braxton replied. "But only when you find a definite and practical way to convert your blindness to an equivalent asset."

With a fresh hit of inspiration, Stovall started attending support groups for blind and visually impaired people. He realized he wasn't alone, despite how lonely some days felt, and discovered that more than 13 million people in the United States shared his affliction, not to mention hundreds of millions more around the world.

Sitting at home one afternoon, out of sheer boredom Stovall put a film into the video player. Although he couldn't see anything, he was able to loosely follow the story based on the dialogue and his memory of having seen it years earlier. During one scene, there was a gunshot and a car noise. But without vision, he had no idea who had been shot and he was no longer able to follow the intended plot line. This left Stovall greatly frustrated with his viewing experience. "Somebody ought to do something about that," he muttered.

At his next support meeting, he shared his experience with a friend, Kathy Harper, who was also legally blind. He shared his sadness that they could no longer watch films or television shows: "If somebody added the voice of a narrator between the dialogue to describe what's going on, blind people could have access to this whole other world of entertainment."

"When are we going to do that?" Harper replied.

"Do what? And who's 'we'? What are you talking about!?"

"Oh…I thought you were actually going to do something about it," she said. "I didn't know you were just talking about it."

Over the next few months, they started to give the idea serious thought. The pair went on a mission to learn all they could about the technical process of film and television production, met with network representatives, and developed a delivery system. In 1988, they founded the Narrative Television Network (NTN).

Within 18 months, the NTN had received an Emmy Award for its pioneering work in making films, television, and educational programming accessible for the visually impaired. It was also rolled out to schools across the country to help visually impaired students access videos on an equal footing with their classmates.

Stovall began to receive invitations for speaking engagements to share his message of hope with people around the world. During one tour, his fellow speakers, Dr. Denis Waitley and Dr. Robert Schuller, asked why he had not yet written a book about his experiences. The next year, his first book, *You Don't Have to Be Blind to See*, was published.

Today, Stovall has written 35 books, including the international bestselling novel *The Ultimate Gift*, which in 2006 was made into a film by 20th Century Fox. He pursued his athletic ambitions as a weightlifter, twice becoming a national champion and qualifying for the 1980 Olympic Games. In 2000, he was chosen as the International Humanitarian of the Year, joining Jimmy Carter, Nancy Reagan, and Mother Teresa as recipients of the honor.

Christopher passed away at the age of seven—the same year he learned to tie his shoes and climb the stairs. Stovall has never forgotten how Christopher inspired him. He remains in contact with Christopher's family and keeps his memory alive as he shares the remarkable story that transformed his own life with audiences around the world. Kathy Harper passed away in 2003, having played a key role in NTN's success.

Stovall still lives in Tulsa and serves as president of the NTN, which now has more than 1,200 broadcast and cable affiliates throughout the world. Above all else, Stovall wants to help people understand that the big dreams lying deep inside their hearts would not have been given to them if they did not have the capacity to achieve them.

Sharon Lechter

"Sharon, have you added value to someone's life today?" Bill asked his daughter. The six-year-old nodded. "Good girl," he said, turning off the light. "See you in the morning."

Bill and his wife, Thelma, were accustomed to moving often. When their two daughters, Sharon and Wanda, were born, the family lived in California, but they soon moved to Illinois and later Florida when Bill called time on his 23-year career in the US Navy. Neither Bill nor Thelma had a college education, although they shared a passion for lifelong learning and making a difference in people's lives. Self-taught, they dreamed that their two daughters would one day receive the college education they missed. Sharon and Wanda were both raised with the belief that they could do anything they set their minds to, with no concession to how females should or shouldn't act.

Complementing the support of her parents with a strong work ethic and desire to help others, Sharon Lechter made it to college, graduating with a degree in accounting. She moved to Atlanta and obtained a job with Coopers & Lybrand, becoming the fourth woman ever hired by a "Big Eight" accounting firm in the southeastern United States. Determination quickly earned

Lechter her CPA certification, but she soon started to feel that if she were working so hard for someone else, perhaps she should do it independently to reap all the rewards and enjoy the freedom to work on whatever she wished. So the 26-year-old left her accountant role and was promptly offered an exciting new opportunity from a former client to cut her entrepreneurial teeth. To evaluate whether this step was the one for her, Lechter sat on her bed and wrote out a list of pros and cons, comfortably arguing both sides. It was a difficult choice, but her pen instinctively scribbled "Why not?" on the pad. That was a more difficult question to answer, and Lechter agreed to start the new venture.

The opportunity looked promising on paper, but it was a complex one. Lechter and her partner hoped to draw on their expertise in accounting and financial management, as well as a new technology, to turn around the business they invested in and restore it to profitability. "At the ripe old age of 26, I thought I knew it all," Lechter reflects. "But it was only when I was knee-deep in the situation that I realized how naïve I'd been." Just a few months in, she discovered numerous improprieties and corruption within the business. With her reputation at stake, and petrified of losing her hard-earned CPA license, she took a week off for some soul searching. When she returned, attorneys were combing through documents in the office, procuring as much evidence as they could find on the business and its operations. However, a silver lining emerged in the form of a suited attorney who was scouring the office, Michael Lechter. Despite their unlikely circumstances, they fell in love and were married nine months later—the worst business decision of Lechter's life had yielded her best outcome. Children would soon follow.

In 1987, Lechter met Zeb Billings, an acclaimed musician who also had established a reputation as an innovator. Billings recruited Lechter to assist with his business, Billings Sight & Sound, and together they revolutionized children's media: they added a plastic piece containing a sound chip to books and board games. Children could simply press a picture on the printed page to hear the musical accompaniment to the nursery rhyme they were reading or to hear characters talk. Lechter recognized from her experiences with her own kids that this more engaging format would attract far more interest in the books and games.

Still, they were wary of resistance to the new technology, so Billings and Lechter entered into a licensing program, partnering with some of the world's most renowned brands, from Disney to Warner Bros. "The first Sesame Street book we put out sold over a million copies," Billings would later note. Sales exploded on the back of the licensing arrangement, reaching $23 million in their fourth year. The company was sold the following year, as sales were projected at a booming $52 million. The project had been a tremendous success, but the experience of leveraging the global brands had

taught Lechter that being the one receiving the royalties and licensing fees was a more lucrative position to
be in.

In December 1992, after the Lechters had moved to
Arizona, their eldest son returned from three months at
college where he confessed, rather sheepishly, to rack-
ing up substantial credit card debt—tallying $2,500 on
credit and eradicating an additional $2,500 from his sav-
ings. "I was pretty mad at him," Lechter remembers,
"but I was angrier with myself because I thought we had
taught him better than that." At a comparable time in
her life, Lechter had saved $22,000 from being finan-
cially responsible and working multiple jobs. Eager to see
where the disconnect occurred, she dug deeper into the
situation and found a big part of the issue lay with how
unscrupulous credit card companies had laid traps for
the students. These companies had used guerrilla marketing campaigns: setting up stalls on college campuses,
attracting attention with free pizza and clothing, then
enticing the students to sign up for high-interest-rate
credit cards under the guise of getting "free cash."
With more research, Lechter realized this was happening at universities across the country. From that point
on, the 38-year-old committed her life to being a financial literacy educator.

A few years later, Lechter's husband phoned to tell
her about a new client, Robert Kiyosaki, who was looking at launching a fun, family-oriented board game

called Cashflow to improve financial literacy for children. Lechter loved the concept, and her background in personal finance and family products meant she had significant expertise to offer, so they joined forces as equal partners in the new venture. As Lechter and Kiyosaki prepared the game for commercialization, they started brainstorming ideas for a brochure that would accompany the game so they could add enough value to justify a high price point. They wrote the brochure together, but the finished product ended up being far more expansive—more of a book. They titled it *Rich Dad Poor Dad*. Feedback from friends and family indicated that the most powerful brand was Rich Dad rather than Cashflow, so they revised their strategy and launched their products.

Both the book and the game became a huge success, striking a chord with parents who were crying out for resources to protect their children from making poor financial decisions and help them take ownership of their lives. In a 10-year period, Lechter and Kiyosaki built the Rich Dad company into a monster brand, writing 15 books together that sold more than 27 million copies in 100 countries and were translated into 51 languages. Individuals and companies around the world contacted the founders, desperate to license the name to spread the message to their own audiences. Finally, Lechter had put herself on the flipside of the licensing deals she had seen from her work with Billings.

In 2007, after achieving more success than they ever imagined, the Rich Dad founders were no longer aligned with their vision for the future, and Lechter made the difficult decision to leave—without any idea what she would do next. It was then that she would learn one of her most profound lessons yet. "I made the decision to do the right thing for me, even if it meant closing what had been such a big chapter in my life. But having faith that there would be a next chapter was one of the most important steps of all." A few months later, Lechter received a phone call from President George W. Bush's office asking her to be on the inaugural President's Advisory Council on Financial Literacy.

Later that year, Don Green, Executive Director of the Napoleon Hill Foundation, called to ask if she'd be interested in some of the projects they had in the pipeline. In 2009, she co-authored the bestselling book *Three Feet from Gold* based on the principle of "never giving up," the core theme of Napoleon Hill's work.

The month it was released, Green contacted Lechter again to let her know about a manuscript that had been in his possession for some time. "In 1938, Hill wrote *Outwitting the Devil* to show readers how to outwit the negativity and fear that we self-sabotage ourselves with," Green said. "But it was never published, in part because Hill's wife was concerned about the title and discouraged its release. Would you take a look at it and let me know what you think?" Lechter read it in its entirety in a single day and called Green back to say the information had to be released to the public and she would be honored to be part of the project. In 2011, the Napoleon Hill Foundation released *Outwitting the Devil* for the first time, annotated by Lechter. In 2014, *Think and Grow Rich for Women* was published, containing real-world advice to help women overcome adversity and seize opportunity.

Today, Sharon Lechter continues her financial literacy crusade. Her efforts have led to change in the state laws of Arizona, where students graduating from high school must now undertake a class in personal finance. As education is state-based, Lechter is still working on the other 49 states. In addition to authoring 22 books, Lechter has worked with the federal government to achieve significant reform in personal finance, including the Credit Card Accountability Responsibility and Disclosure Act of 2009, a federal statute passed by the United States Congress and signed by President Barack Obama that, among other things, prohibits credit card companies from soliciting students on college campuses. "Keep the faith," Lechter says of her remarkable success. "You never know what phone call can change your life!"

Sharon and Michael Lechter have been happily married for 37 years and use all the resources at their disposal to give young people the tools they need to succeed. Each night, Lechter still asks herself how she added value to people's lives that day.

AUTO-
SUGGESTION

THE MEDIUM FOR INFLUENCING
THE SUBCONSCIOUS MIND

*"There are no limitations to the mind
except those that we acknowledge."*
—NAPOLEON HILL

ONCE YOU UNDERSTAND AND CAN APPLY THE POWER of the mind, you wield a truly infinite force. You can bend the rules of the game to your advantage, not only controlling the present, but the future and the past, too. Since the subconscious mind is not inspired by indifference, it stands to reason that any success we want in our lives must be packaged as a burning desire delivered through the emotion of faith to our subconscious. Auto-suggestion is the agent between the conscious and the subconscious, which can be manipulated through the right stimulus.

All humans have ultimate control over what reaches our mind. We experience life through our five senses, generating thoughts in our consciousness, which we can then reject or accept to enter into our subconscious. But the great majority of people do not exercise this control, going through life without any filter over what enters the mind—the most sacred of possessions. However, the few who do, experience prosperity beyond their wildest imagination.

Visualizing the object of your desires—whether that be a full bank account, a successful business, or a loving marriage—is not enough. Clearly state what you want, see it already in your possession, feel every associated emotion, and outline what you are willing to do—the price you are willing to pay—in exchange for its attainment. At least twice daily, confidently read the written statement of your desire out loud.

A challenging lesson for today's generations, who live in an increasingly fast-paced world, is learning and appreciating that there is no such thing as something for nothing. Success appears only to those who have paid the price, in advance and in full. Roger Federer turned the consistent action of hitting millions of tennis balls into more Grand Slam titles than any other male player in history and significant personal wealth.

Through constant repetition of your desire, reinforced with absolute faith in its attainment, your orders are converted to the necessary daily actions. Lasting success does not emerge unless the price—the faith, imagination, hard work, and persistence—is paid. Only you can decide whether the end result is worthy of the enduring sacrifice required.

Through the process of auto-suggestion, you must convince your subconscious that it's a simple choice: win or perish. Demand success, expect it, and let the universe show you the way forward.

Bob Proctor

Growing up in Toronto, Canada, 26-year-old Robert Proctor tried his hand at everything that crossed his path. His current job, working at a fire hall in the center of town, was the latest in a string of menial jobs that kept him living paycheck to paycheck.

One day, he met an elegantly dressed man who ran the company next door. They built a rapport, and he asked Proctor questions he had never heard before. The man pointed out three areas—happiness, health, and wealth—and asked him to rank his success in each. Proctor thought he was happy, healthy, and wealthy enough, but at that stage in his life, he didn't realize just how low he'd set the bar. Growing up on the tail end of the Depression, and then the Second World War, he never imagined that a better life awaited if he were ready to receive it.

"Listen to me. If you read that book and do exactly what I tell you, you can have anything you want," the man said, pointing to a copy of *Think and Grow Rich* on the nearby table.

Aside from required texts in school, Proctor had very little reading experience—not even comic books. Like many kids his age, he'd grown up in a household struggling to make ends meet while the men were away in

Europe as part of the Commonwealth forces fighting for freedom. Proctor had left school at age 15, feeling he needed a job more than an education. But with only low-level schooling and no business experience, he fell into a cycle of dead-end jobs that provided only meager wages. Ten years on, Proctor was a man going nowhere.

But the immense conviction of the enigmatic businessman made him sufficiently curious. He read the book, becoming completely engrossed by its contents, especially the anecdotes from the most successful people who ever lived, and vowed to act.

His first step, as the man demonstrated, was to write down what he wanted on a goal card and carry that with him everywhere he went. Proctor wrote that he would have $25,000 by New Year's Day of 1970. Previously, he had settled for whatever fortune came his way; this was the first time he actively and consciously chased the money he wanted.

"I gave myself a decade to do it," Proctor later reflected, "but I really didn't believe it was going to happen. As I kept reading the book, I found out what happened. If you read something often enough, you'll start to believe it."

He met a man, Al Phillips, who mentioned there was good money cleaning offices, but with one condition: "If you're going to do it, do it for yourself—not for somebody else." At that time, if you cleaned floors for a company you were paid around $1 an hour. The company, however, charged $10–$20 per hour. Proctor borrowed a thousand dollars, then bought two secondhand cleaning machines, plus several buckets and mops. He was in business.

With the goal card still in his pocket, Proctor went forth. He worked around the clock and always kept an eye out for any new offices that he could clean. Eventually his exertions caught up with him and he collapsed on the street. He woke to find a burly policeman closely staring at him, with a crowd of people behind. After a few deep breaths, Proctor gingerly stood up and walked home.

The aspiring entrepreneur knew something was wrong with how he was carrying out his plans and worried about what would happen to his burgeoning business with him out of commission. His inner voice whispered, "If you can't clean all of them, don't clean any of them." Proctor hired a team of cleaners to do all the work, and his business thrived. Over the next 12 months he earned more than $200,000 and established cleaning contracts in Toronto, Montreal, Boston, Cleveland, Atlanta, and London. A few years later, he crossed the million-dollar turnover mark. With every success, his ambitions skyrocketed. Proctor smiled—his goal card would need updating.

A friend, Harrold Rose, introduced him to audio recordings of influential figures in the sales, motivation, and leadership fields. Proctor was instantly captivated by Earl Nightingale, the radio personality and author of *The Strangest Secret*. Nightingale had also narrated a condensed version of *Think and Grow Rich*, which Proctor bought and played frequently.

Determined to meet his new idol, who at the time was just a voice (albeit the most successful voice in the history of broadcasting), Proctor plucked up his courage and picked up the phone. He was pleasantly surprised to get through to the man himself. After some persistence, Proctor made an appointment to meet Nightingale face to face in Chicago.

They met for an hour, and Proctor was fascinated. He decided before he even left Nightingale's office that he would come back to work for him and learn his secrets firsthand. Proctor sold his cleaning empire and moved to Chicago to start his next chapter, earning a mere $18,000 a year. "I would have paid them to let me work there," he justified.

For the next few years, he learned as much as he could from Nightingale and his business partner, Lloyd Conant. To align his growth with theirs, Proctor paid their secretary to keep him in the loop on anything related to success or personal development: if they bought a book, he would be told what it was so he could get the same one; if they subscribed to a magazine, he would too; if someone important was stopping by, Proctor would get a heads-up so he could emerge at just the right time.

With his unparalleled eagerness to learn, coupled with superior relationship-building skills, Bob Proctor was elevated to vice president of sales in four years, and his salary doubled.

One day Proctor approached Conant, suggesting they stop selling the recordings that had underpinned the company's revenue for years. At that time, they were selling a 12-pack of 7-inch discs and cassettes for $245, an exorbitant purchase compared to long-playing records that retailed for 50 cents. Proctor had realized that the value was not in the recordings but in the action spawned from the recordings. Since most people bought the recordings and never did anything with them, they needed another level of support.

"We should give them the cassette and sell them a seminar," Proctor proposed.

Conant laughed and said, "I don't think so, Bob. We're staying in the cassette business. We'll leave the seminar business to Dale Carnegie."

Proctor had an inkling it was time to move on. He would forever be grateful for that period of his life, but he felt the need to tread his own path again. He committed to creating a seminar series that would give people all they needed to make positive and sustainable changes in their lives. No longer would they be constrained by the limited belief system that had chipped away at their dreams since childhood. Bob Proctor wanted to inspire the world—to help anyone achieve whatever success they wanted—and now he had a plan to do it. He put together the seminar series and got to work on its promotion.

Each series would include a weekly workshop for eight weeks, and the room would cater for up to 100 attendees. As Proctor and his team prepared for their first event, the head of training for IBM, one of the world's largest computer consulting companies, dropped by inquisitively. With interest from the corporate sector, Proctor thought, perhaps the seminar series would take off even quicker than he had imagined.

But at the first event, he walked on stage to a lone attendee. One hundred seats had been set, and the room felt very empty. Dejected but undeterred, Proctor delivered his material as if there were a capacity crowd.

Over time, word started to spread, and Proctor was able to arrange a meeting with Mel Haycraft, vice president of sales for Prudential Insurance Company of America. It was 1974, and Prudential—founded a century earlier—was one of the world's largest insurance companies, with more than 20,000 employees. Haycraft presided over the best performing territory, by far, in the company.

As they spoke, Haycraft failed to identify any value in what Proctor was offering compared to the myriad other courses that promised superior results. Finally, Haycraft asked, "Why is your program different?"

"Because I'm different," Proctor said. "I'll make you a deal. Give me one hundred of your best people. Don't give me the worst—anybody can do something with them. Give me a hundred of your *best* people. I'll give you a one-day seminar for free, and I assure you, you'll see results."

With Proctor's personal guarantee, the seminar went ahead. It was so well received that he was invited to speak with the rest of the staff. The following month, in a room of 450 people, he started his presentation with the bold claim: "I can show *anyone* here how to write $5 million." Whispers filled the room. The group seemed less responsive compared to the previous Prudential seminars.

At the break, an audience member, Don Slovin, asked Proctor if he had ever sold insurance before.

"No, never. Why do you ask?" Proctor replied.

"You don't know what the hell you're talking about," Slovin asserted. "You said anyone in this room could write $5 million. Do you know we've never had anyone in the history of the company write $5 million in a year?"

"You could be the first," Proctor offered.

"But you said we could do it this year, and the year's more than halfway over."

"Then it isn't going to take you as long, is it?" Proctor said.

By the end of December, just four months later, Slovin closed the year having written more than $6 million in new business. A number of the others to whom Proctor had spoken had joined the $5 million club and were at his heels. Proctor had led them to question their beliefs and interpretation of what was possible; in doing so, he had completely redefined how one of the world's largest insurance companies viewed success.

From his own humble beginnings, Bob Proctor saw how repetition and the continual study of human potential had completely transformed his happiness, health, and wealth. Today, and until his last breath, his mission to elevate people above their own circumstances continues.

Satish Verma

"Satish, would you like to see a movie with me?" Krishna Lal asked his great-nephew.

"What's a movie?" the seven-year-old replied.

Satish Verma had spent his short life growing up in the slums of Ferozepur in northern India during one of the most tumultuous periods in the country's history. In 1947, when the British government transferred control back to India after almost a century of rule, a power struggle had broken out, forcing much of the country into bloody conflict, leading to millions of deaths and the displacement of millions more. On the border between India and the soon-to-be-formed Pakistan, Ferozepur was one of the regions most affected. During the power struggle, protests poured through the streets and violent confrontations decimated the city. The boy's father, a respected physician within the community, was killed in the riots, leaving behind a wife and three children, including his newborn son, Satish.

With the searing tensions in the city and the loss of their father, the family soon had to move from their home into the slums. Totally illiterate and thrust into the urgent role of family breadwinner, Verma's mother washed soiled diapers from the children of local families to help put food on the table. Despite the hardship, the family never saw their situation as more than a temporary adversity. "These days won't last long," Verma's mother frequently reassured her children.

As the country began to settle, their lives returned to a new normal. And it was then that Verma's great-uncle took him to see his very first movie. While the film played, the boy became enamored with the main character despite not being able to understand the English dialogue. As the projector whirred, a scene unfolded where the film's protagonist was enjoying a coffee with a beautiful blonde woman in Switzerland. Verma sat mesmerized—by the charismatic hero, the woman with a hair color unlike anything he'd ever seen before, and the elegant location. The film unveiled a world he had not known existed, and the scene would never leave his mind. "One day I'll visit that place," he promised himself.

During his teenage years, Verma focused hard on his schoolwork and was accepted into college, where he studied psychology and literature. During his studies, he became fascinated with the world outside India—Europe in particular. His diligence led to excellent grades, and he applied for a graduate program in Canada and was accepted on a full scholarship. Better yet, the university promised to pay his travel and living expenses, too. The 23-year-old met with the travel agent, who would book his flight to Toronto with just one request: Was there any way the flight could stop in Switzerland, even if just for a day, so he could visit the restaurant from the film that had been imprinted on his mind for 16 years? With some creative thinking, the agent booked the flight to Toronto in a way that would be near impossible for him to make his connection in Zürich, leaving the airline to cover his accommodation and auxiliary costs until the next flight to Toronto departed the following day. Verma packed all his things into a small bag, collected his eight dollars in savings—all the money he had in the world—said farewell to his family, and set off on his adventure.

As planned, he missed the connection to Toronto, and the airline provided one night's accommodation, as well as food and transportation costs, for a 23-hour stay in Zürich. Verma dropped his bag at the hotel, then asked the front desk attendant, first, if there was a river in the city, and second, if there was a coffee shop overlooking it. "Yes, the Limmat River," the attendant replied, "but we have many coffee shops."

Verma quickly paced along the river until he found the scene from the film. Sitting down at the table, he peeled off a dollar bill and placed his order with the waitress. As the aroma of roasted coffee beans met his nostrils, he pressed the cup to his lips. "If I can leave the slum in India to track down this coffee shop in Switzerland with only eight dollars, I can do *anything*," he thought. It had been a dream 16 years in the making, but it reassured Verma that with passion, hard work, and the right plan, the universe would deliver.

Landing in Canada, he made his connecting flight to Thunder Bay and began his graduate studies in literature. Outside the classroom, Verma worked as a kitchen assistant in a busy sandwich restaurant that boasted three locations throughout the city. Though it was hard work, he enjoyed making friends and learning about a new industry. The restaurant was popular, but several years into his tenure, two professionals in suits strolled in and asked to see the owner. "He's not here," Verma replied. "We haven't seen him for a few days." From the ensuing conversation, the 29-year-old learned that, despite strong sales, the restaurant was in great financial strife because numerous bills had been ignored due to the owner's spiraling gambling habits. The bank had run out of patience, sending two of their representatives to either recoup the outstanding debts or shut the business down.

"They seem like popular locations. Why don't you buy the business?" one of the bankers asked. Despite knowing as well as anybody how the business operated, Verma pointed out that he was a student and simply could not afford to make the payments. "All you need to do is pay us $100 per month," the bankers reassured him. He discussed it with a friend who also worked at the restaurant, and they agreed to split ownership in half, each paying $50 per month to save the business. In 1976, five years after starting work there as a kitchen assistant, Satish Verma officially became a restauranteur. That year, he brought in more than $20,000. "It was a lot of money in those days," Verma laughs as he recalls his first foray into entrepreneurship.

He returned to India for an arranged marriage, meeting his bride-to-be, Anita, on a Sunday and marrying her that Wednesday. The couple returned to Canada, had two children, and enjoyed a life far removed from the poverty and squalor of Verma's own upbringing. As his income continued to rise, he diversified his investments into real estate. One day, he was approached with a business concept that would roll out a new style of pizza restaurant and promised to open locations nationwide. At that juncture, Verma was a much more seasoned restauranteur and had a dream to own a global restaurant chain. The deal felt right and oozed potential, so he sold his share in the sandwich restaurant business, as well as the equity from his growing real estate portfolio, to free up as much money as he could. That gave him $500,000 of investment capital, but he met with the bank and borrowed an additional $500,000 so his contribution to the pizza concept would be an even $1 million, for a chance of much higher returns.

At first he was excited for the new venture, but his hope quickly turned to fear as the project began to falter. A few months in, it was clear that the pizza venture was an unmitigated disaster—Verma then realized he had been fleeced of every penny he invested. "Imagine losing everything in a business venture, going through bankruptcy, having a huge debt with no income, and two young children and a wife to support," he says. "It was the most challenging period in my life." A single ill-advised decision had damning repercussions, leaving but one haunting question: "What do I do now?" All he had left from a lifetime of work was $500 cash in his personal bank account. After the initial shock, he remembered what his mother repeated to him and his brothers in the Ferozepur slums: "These days won't last long."

Using more than half of the remaining funds in his account, Verma enrolled in a $300 course on success that was offered via correspondence from the Napoleon Hill Foundation's head office in Illinois. They would mail out the course materials to each participant, who would complete the coursework and return it for feedback. "People thought I was crazy for investing more than half of my remaining net worth in a course," Verma remembers. "But at a time when so many people around me were trying to point out where I went wrong, I listened to my inner self and went to work planning what I could do *right*."

The first lesson he received was *Definiteness of Purpose*. As he read through the course materials, Verma learned about the stories of all those who had succeeded despite tremendous adversity, with many of them going bankrupt before reaching their crowning glory. "If they can do it, I can do it too," he told himself, with dogged determination.

Combing through the course materials, one particular passage stood out: *Whatever the mind can conceive and believe, it can achieve.* Verma felt it might be time to put the author's teachings through the ultimate test, as he conceived his most ambitious goal yet—to be out of his bankruptcy within six months. "If what Napoleon Hill says is true," he thought, "this will happen." He also vowed to one day work with, or alongside, the Napoleon Hill Foundation.

To help the universe along with his goals, Verma hurriedly but comprehensively worked out a plan to give himself the best chance of success. He invited Bob, an acquaintance who worked at one of the top-rated banks in town, out to lunch. Due to their relationship, the banker approved Verma for a credit card that would help him put food on the table for his family and provide other resources for him to restart his professional services career, this time focusing on psychology and education. Six months later, after a frugal period of hard work and creative thinking, Verma had achieved his goal. Shortly after, he was able to purchase a home for Anita and their two children. His professional services career continued to expand, and he would eventually sell the business for over $1 million. Having personally witnessed the power of Hill's teachings, Verma promised that he would spend the rest of his life sharing Hill's success principles and message of prosperity with the world.

Knowing that *Think and Grow Rich* was one of the most successful books of all time, with more than 100 million copies sold, Verma pondered why there weren't more success stories like his. After all, he had been born during significant turmoil, grew up in a slum without a father, and left the country with eight dollars to his name—but had been able to realize his childhood dream of visiting Switzerland and become a successful businessman twice over. He attributed it to two reasons: one, readers didn't understand the book, or, two, they didn't put it into action. Verma shared his thoughts with the Napoleon Hill Foundation and, in 2013, he founded the Think and Grow Rich Institute in Toronto to help people of all backgrounds apply Hill's teachings to improve their own lives. In partnership with the Foundation, the Institute is committed to keeping the *Think and Grow Rich* legacy alive. "I don't sleep because I'm so excited to make a difference in the lives of millions of people," Verma says. "If you're not giving back, what's the point of being on the earth?"

In his limited spare time, Satish Verma travels the world sharing his remarkable story about never giving in, no matter how dire your circumstances appear. It's his hope that future generations understand that everything they need to succeed is already within them: that they are always in total control of their destiny. "When you control your thoughts, you enjoy every moment," he explains, "because every moment can be a defining moment in your life."

SPECIALIZED KNOWLEDGE

PERSONAL EXPERIENCES
OR OBSERVATIONS

*"Knowledge is only potential power. It
becomes power only when, and if, it is
organized into definite plans of action,
and directed to a definite end."*
—NAPOLEON HILL

KNOWLEDGE—LIKE IDEAS—IS MEANINGLESS BY itself. However, acquiring specialized knowledge and then learning to organize it into a definite plan of action, directing it to a specific end, and developing the faith to see it through is true power. This far supersedes the much more lauded quality of intellect or book-smarts. Indeed, for educated people, knowing how to convert their knowledge into wealth is far more elusive than most admit. The focus we place on continually acquiring knowledge should be on an equal footing with continually *applying* that knowledge, which is the gateway to everyone on earth realizing their potential.

Those who orient their lives toward success shift their daily routine to make the continual application of specialized knowledge a habit. Just as compound interest can be a powerful servant or a cruel master, so too can habits either exponentially help or hinder our progress. Too many people fall victim to bad habits, letting ongoing distractions muffle their inner voice and leaving them indifferent to their own success. Contrast this with those who enjoy good habits—thinking positive thoughts, surrounding themselves with winners, applying what they learn, nurturing their desire as a burning obsession, and paying the price each day for their future success.

Consult your definite purpose and you will quickly identify the foundation of knowledge you need to achieve your goal. Then, use the tremendous resources at your disposal to start your life's work. Today, you not only have the same book stores, libraries, and universities that previous generations enjoyed, but also instant access to billions of people and the infinite knowledge of civilization through technology. Never has it been easier to acquire what you need to become a success. Technology has torn down barriers to entry for almost all industries and leveled the playing field in countless ways. With the right mindset, opportunity exists wherever we look.

Education is not predicated on what school or university you attend. True education, in a practical sense, is your ability to source specialized knowledge and direct it toward the achievement of a definite purpose. History has proven time and time again that those who know how to apply specialized knowledge enjoy far greater success, irrespective of industry, than those of superior intellect. After almost a decade of computer programming experience, Mark Zuckerberg combined his specialized knowledge with the talents of others to launch social networking monolith, Facebook, making him one of the richest people in the world in his early thirties.

Using your definite purpose, acquire the knowledge you need, and then organize it in a way that enables you to add significant value to other people's lives as payment for your own future success.

Lewis Howes

Lewis Howes smiled at his opponent. The 25-year-old wide receiver had been a revelation for the Cleveland Browns NFL team throughout the 2007 season.

Howes had put in thousands of hours off the field that led to a dominant performance on it—ferocious training to get in the best physical shape of his life, continual reading of the playbook to give the Browns a host of offensive options, and persistently watching game reels to know rival teams inside and out.

Now, playing in front of his home crowd in Cleveland, Ohio, Howes needed one more touchdown to equal the single game club record. It would be the defining moment of his career.

The Patriots' defensive team scrambled, desperate to stem the flow of points from the barnstorming Browns. As the line of scrimmage formed, wide receiver Howes—with laser-like focus—knew exactly where he needed to be.

The play started, and BANG. Howes winced and fell to the ground.

The bright lights and roaring crowd faded into emptiness. As his eyes adjusted to the darkness, reality hit. It had all been a dream, a dream that refused to die. A cruel hoax of his subconscious that kept his NFL dream alive long after hope had been extinguished.

Howes gingerly sat up on the worn sofa in his sister's living room, his bed for the last year. Sleep had been scarce since his wrist injury, which required a surgical procedure to transplant bone from his hip to his fractured wrist. Standing six foot four inches tall, no sofa was ever going to be comfortable, and the cast covering his arm from hand to shoulder added another level of frustration.

For as long as he could remember, Howes's dream had been to play in the NFL, but the devastating wrist injury had put the brakes on a promising football career.

Growing up dyslexic, Howes naturally gravitated to anything that didn't require paper or a pencil. He enjoyed watching how practice united the team for a common goal and found sports an easy way to make the friendships that eluded him in elementary school.

Howes's father served as an early mentor for the impressionable teen, even if it did take a while to grasp the alchemy in his father's methods. Howes reflects: "My father would never celebrate my birthday, but one day I understood why. He didn't ever want me to focus on age because of the limitations it imposed. Free of that crutch, he hoped to equip me with the mindset that I could do anything."

In his fourth year of college, after transferring schools, Lewis Howes first found the sporting recognition he craved—he was named an All-American athlete, albeit in the decathlon. As he had never officially trained for the decathlon, it was a welcome accomplishment for the 22-year-old.

One year later, he was named an All-American in football, too. He felt accepted and validated. His lofty NFL goal even seemed attainable.

NFL scouts gave the ambitious Ohioan a chance, but looking around at how fast, strong, and brawny his competition was, Howes suspected he might never make it to the next level. With the faintest hope remaining, he signed with a team in the Arena Football League that valued his competitiveness, discipline, and do-or-die attitude.[1]

The following season, he crashed into the perimeter wall during a game, and his wrist bore the brunt of the impact. Scans showed the wrist was too frail to put screws in, instead requiring a bone graft to stabilize the area. Six months in a full-length arm cast, followed by another year of physical therapy, would complete the healing process. While his arm would recover, his football dream would not.

Sport was the only thing in which Howes felt he had natural talent. With no income, college degree, or career prospects, he began to rack up substantial credit card debt and struggled with depression. "It was the lowest

---

1 The Arena Football League is a professional indoor football league in the United States. It is played on a smaller field with less mainstream exposure and much lower player wages than the NFL.

low I've ever experienced," he remembers. For months he laid on his sister's couch staring at the ceiling, pondering where it had all gone so horribly wrong.

He reflected on his dad's advice—that he could do anything he wanted—but that just confused him more. One day it hit him like a football to the chest: yes, he could do anything he wanted, but that formula was incomplete. Throughout his entire life, every accomplishment, regardless of how small, was due to the assistance, collaboration, or influence of others. To rise above his circumstances—the meager bank balance, crippling injury, and makeshift bed—he needed a coach. Only this time, the stakes were much higher: the game of *life*.

Given his sporting background, Howes understood that coaches valued players with specialized skills. So, like a character in a video game, he began to build up his stats in areas that were essential to success in the business world. At the same time, he put himself in as many situations as he could to cross paths with accomplished individuals. His burning desire to transcend his circumstances led him to read books that were credited with shaping the leaders of the last century, and he complemented that by actively building familiarity with the digital networking platform LinkedIn.

Drawing on his uncomfortable experience as a stay-at-home patient, Howes conceived a new product that would be a more functional version of the full-length cast. To help develop this idea, he sought out a local inventor who had experience with refining products and bringing them to market. After months of persistent requests from an eager Howes, the inventor agreed to help. While the product was never brought to market, it taught him valuable lessons in idea generation, design, packaging, positioning, marketing, and product development that would be a tremendous asset.

A few weeks later, while attending a networking event, he met a man who had forged a lucrative career on the speaking circuit. "Wait a minute...you get paid to speak?" Howes asked, incredulous. The 24-year-old's eyes were opening to a world he never knew existed.

"You need to join Toastmasters so you can learn the art of public speaking," the speaker advised him. "Master the skills—structure, vocal variety, and body language—before you become a presenter."

"But I'm terrified to speak in public," Howes thought.

However, his desire to succeed outweighed his fear. Every week for the next year, Howes showed up to Toastmasters and practiced speech after speech. Through purposeful repetition of a skill that was far outside his comfort zone, things began to change; one of his greatest fears transmuted into both a strength and a passion.

Howes set a goal: to make $5,000 in a speech by the end of the year. "I had no clue how it was going to happen, but I had a vision, a coach, and a game plan that I executed every single week," he recounts.

The Toastmasters meetings proved to be a fruitful opportunity to meet other ambitious people in the community. Howes was awestruck by one speaker, Frank Agin, who dazzled the group every time. One day Howes approached him and asked if he could take him out to lunch to learn how he became so successful.

"I would love to learn how you got to where you are!" Howes said.

Throughout his self-transformation, Howes asked people how they had become successful, rather than directly asking people for advice. He found this way he quickly received honest information from proven people across various fields.

Aside from being an exceptional orator, Agin was a bestselling author and networking expert. They both shared their stories, and Agin asked if Howes would use his LinkedIn expertise to help him grow his online business.

Afterward, Agin gave Howes a $100 check for his services—another lightbulb moment for the aspiring entrepreneur: "I could get paid to teach someone a skill that I myself was learning?"

This reinforced Howes's belief in broadening his skill set as efficiently as he could. His rapidly expanding network of coaches and mentors also offered the growth—via challenge, structure, and feedback—that kept him disciplined enough to focus on constant improvement. Eventually, Howes started to be recognized as a person of value in the business world.

LinkedIn had proved to be an increasingly useful tool, and soon he connected with thousands of people quickly and without any financial outlay. With a gentle push from his mentors, Howes monetized this asset by creating and selling one-on-one online consultations in which he would help individuals and small businesses craft the perfect profile to generate more leads. His clients were satisfied with the results, and word-of-mouth referrals started to trickle in. Seeing how pleased his clients were with the value he added to their businesses, and limited by the number of hours in a day, Howes raised his prices. Interest in his consultations continued to climb, and he continually searched for ways he could add more value to his clients.

Agin, impressed with Howes's digital acumen, suggested they write a book together—a quintessential guide to real-world and online networking principles. Having almost flunked out of English in high school, he took some convincing, but as Howes's mentor, Agin assured him of two things: first, he would help him every step of the way; and second, the juice would be worth the squeeze. At age 25, Lewis Howes—the washed-up athlete who only learned to properly read and write as a senior in high school—was an author.

Brimming with confidence after this experience, he partnered with an IT specialist and plotted a way to amplify his message for a mass audience. With his partner doing everything on the tech side and Howes promoting and delivering the sessions, they hosted webinars for people around the world. As social media marketing flourished, so too did their business. Three years later, Howes sold his share of the business, netting him his first significant financial windfall.

With some money now at his disposal, and to capitalize on his growing profile, Howes decided the time was right to move in a different direction—the *School of Greatness* podcast. Audible content had grown sharply in popularity in the few years prior, and the budding entrepreneur wanted to use the platform to interview industry leaders so he could share their secrets for the world to benefit. Along the way, he would receive exclusive access to a constant stream of inspirational professionals.

At the time of writing, his personal website attracts 200,000 visitors each month, and his *School of Greatness* podcast has amassed 25 million downloads. Howes still makes time for at least one webinar a week, which over the last eight years have brought in more than $10 million in sales. In 2016 he released the *School of Greatness* book, which quickly became a *New York Times* bestseller, and he has more books in the pipeline.

For all his success, he's quick to correct people who confuse action with intellect. "I just wasn't afraid," Howes said. "I was so ignorant and had no clue what to do, so I would just act. Like in sports, I thought about my vision, found a coach and mentor, and got to work on a game plan. Above all else, action...every single day."

Today, Lewis Howes remains focused on sharing the struggles and learnings of the world's most accomplished people to inspire a generation. Seeds of greatness are often sown during our darkest hours, but those who take the time to think about their vision, stay committed to growth, and are willing to step outside their comfort zone have an opportunity to live the richest lives of all.

Noel Whittaker

In 1986, on the outskirts of Brisbane, Australia, Noel Whittaker evaluated his finances. Something didn't add up.

He reflected on his journey to that point. He had tried hard in high school but never achieved outstanding grades. He had been the laughing stock of woodwork class and the last picked in sporting teams.

Whittaker's parents had instilled in him the importance of being a good, honest worker. However, they had been scarred by the Great Depression of 1929 and urged him to take a safe job that provided a stable income. They were also class conscious. His father left school at the age of 14 and had spent his life working as a live-in farm manager. The family did not own any property and money was short, but they enjoyed their lives. Whittaker and his younger brother were expected to help with all the daily chores and learned the value of teamwork and the importance of putting in the effort before expecting the results.

In a misguided attempt to insulate their two children from life's disappointments, Whittaker's parents warned them that anybody from their background should not expect to progress too far up the ladder of success.

Deep inside, Whittaker had a burning desire to "be somebody." All his favorite books had heroes in them, and he fantasized that one day he would stand out from the crowd, too. But with nothing to give him direction, his desires floundered.

After graduating from high school, he obtained a job as a teller with Westpac, Australia's oldest bank. He felt comfortable knowing that he would be better positioned than most in the event of another depression. Whittaker's work ethic held him in good stead, and he slowly climbed the ranks.

Eventually, a law firm enticed him away from his secure job at the bank, and he joined their growing team. A clash of personalities led to an argument between him and the managing partner. In a fit of temper, just three weeks before Christmas, Whittaker resigned from the law firm. He then learned the hard way that very few companies hire in December or January. With each failed employment application, he became increasingly disheartened.

His worst fears had been realized. Just two months shy of his thirtieth birthday, Noel Whittaker had no job and no income.

"I vividly remember sitting in the kitchen alone, sobbing," he reflects. "My life had no direction, no purpose, and—I thought—no hope."

Whittaker bounced between jobs for a few years until he finally got a position at a finance company, becoming responsible for joint venture subdivisions. He found the job particularly galling because any ideas he proposed were ignored. It was a bureaucracy of pettiness and politics, and he felt trapped.

Whittaker, now 35 years old, was bursting with ideas and ambition, but totally frustrated.

As fate would have it, the finance company offered an audiocassette version of *Think and Grow Rich* to all their staff. This single action stopped him in his tracks. He played the tape over and over, then rushed out to buy a secondhand copy of the book—the only one he could find. As he eagerly highlighted passages, his mind lit up. It would be one of the best investments he would ever make.

For the first time, Whittaker realized that all his limitations were self-imposed. Changing his thoughts would give him complete freedom to take control of his life.

He made two promises: first, he would start his own business within 100 days; second, he would spend the rest of his life promulgating Napoleon Hill's success principles.

Just a few days behind schedule, Whittaker and a friend started their own construction and real estate company. As an additional service to clients, they eventually diversified into mortgage brokering, which then expanded into a successful financial planning business.

After 10 years of growth, he felt set for life.

Out of left field, an opportunity beckoned, and Whittaker hoped it would be his ticket to much greater wealth. An experienced property developer approached him and his business partner to see if they would be interested in building a neighborhood shopping center together.

The plan was simple: buy a commercial block of land, build the center, and attract a bevy of quality retailers, boutique shops, and staple stores. They would receive long-term rental income that would increase in the coming years as more people moved into the area. At the time, residential and commercial properties in the region had achieved steady growth—doubling in value about every nine years—so the opportunity for the increase in land value only added to the appeal.

In hindsight, there were warning signs. The property developer had gone bankrupt from previous failed developments and was thus unable to obtain financing for the "incredible opportunity." The trio agreed that Whittaker and his partner would borrow the cash in their names. There was a further problem. If the venture failed, the losses would be met by Whittaker and his business partner. If it succeeded, the profits would be split between all three of them. They borrowed $1 million, funded by progressive drawdowns as the center was built. In line with standard practice at the time, interest was added directly to the principal.

To make the development a success, they would need to: prepare plans for a shopping center that would attract interest from a wide range of prospective tenants and customers; agree to leasing terms with each tenant; and, above all, manage their cashflow carefully to keep the development afloat.

Property development is notoriously high risk and dependent on many factors. But one of the most important elements is the skill of the developers themselves to oversee the hundreds of small tasks that are needed to make the project worthwhile. So, the trio used the common strategy of commissioning their architect to manage the project: to literally create the blueprint and monitor the progress to ensure it aligned with the developers' expectations.

As construction on their ambitious venture started, the market turned. A credit squeeze meant that finance was extremely difficult to obtain, regardless of income. Interest rates skyrocketed to their highest-ever levels, leaving Whittaker and his partner paying 22% interest on their loan. More than $4,000 in interest was being added to the loan each *week*.

Pressure started to mount.

With construction nearing completion, Whittaker and his business partner realized that the architect whom the developer had hired was incompetent. Design faults riddled the development: the ceiling of the designated bakery space did not reach the minimum height to accommodate essential machinery and equipment, and only a front entry had been made for the proposed butcher shop when, by law, it also required a rear entry.

Like dining at an empty restaurant, no one wanted to be the first tenant to sign a lease, especially in a development that failed to offer the adequate space needed to operate their business. Once word of the disaster had spread, the prospective tenants on their call lists would remain just that.

Whittaker retreated to his home office for some soul searching. He questioned his decisions up to that point and lamented, "Why did I even entertain such a high-risk venture?"

The gamble had been unsuccessful, and his faith was about to be tested like never before.

He clumsily tapped numbers into the calculator, trying to estimate how long it would take before his family—a wife, two young children, and a baby—would be forced out of their home and their assets decimated.

In despair, he fell to the floor of his home office and prayed.

The next morning, Whittaker broached the very difficult discussion with his wife, Geraldine. She responded with unexpected positivity: "I don't care if we lose the house, just don't lose your good name—that's the most important thing."

That conversation helped Whittaker reframe the situation and reminded him that there's always a way if you look hard enough.

In the next few weeks, Whittaker sold almost all the assets he had spent a lifetime acquiring. While it was an extraordinarily difficult decision, it allowed him to keep the family home by the slimmest of margins. That eased the pressure of the snowballing debt, and the disastrous shopping center was sold for much less than it cost a few months later.

It had been a spectacular failure and a very, very expensive lesson.

Justifiably hesitant about further property developments, Whittaker focused all his efforts on the financial planning business. He started writing personal finance articles for regional newspapers and began to make a name for himself on local radio.

He resolved to write a book that could help others achieve happiness and financial independence. Whittaker merged his financial planning knowledge with the Napoleon Hill teachings that had been so pivotal in how he viewed the world. The manuscript was rejected by dozens of publishers, but at that point in his life the 46-year-old knew that there was always a way if he persisted. Finally, in 1987 a publisher relented, on the condition that Whittaker cover all the costs and thus bear all the risk.

Making Money Made Simple was born.

Whittaker set an audacious target: to sell 100,000 copies in the first year of its release. He would travel the country tirelessly, doing whatever it took to spread the word and achieve his goal.

Almost 30 years later, more than two million copies of *Making Money Made Simple* have been sold, and it has become a major bestseller in Australia, New Zealand, South Africa, and the United Kingdom. Since he'd taken all the risk, the subsequent rewards—the book royalties—were strongly in his favor. In 2001, the book was named one of the "100 Most Influential Books of the 20th Century." It also attracted thousands of prospective clients to his financial planning business, which grew to be the largest of its type in Australia.

In 2011, Whittaker was honored with an Order of Australia for his services to financial education. Finally, Noel Whittaker had made it.

In his most catastrophic failure, the seeds of greatness were sown. The expensive lesson was worth every penny.

IMAGINATION
THE WORKSHOP OF THE MIND

"If you never see great riches in your imagination, you will never see them in your bank balance."
—NAPOLEON HILL

IMAGINATION IS THE PRECURSOR, THE ROCKET fuel, for your plans, as well as the link between desire and action. All great innovations through time can be attributed to imagination. Today, we have planes that can safely fly across the world in less than a day, hand-held devices that allow high-definition video calling to anyone for free, commercial civilian travel to outer space, and lightning-fast access to any information we need through the internet. Yet they all were once just sparks of human imagination. As with knowledge, imagination is superfluous if not acted upon and directed toward a definite purpose.

Ultimate self-mastery, and its subsequent rewards, requires that we not only allow the success spark to enter our consciousness, but that we fan the flames. Unfortunately, too many people spend more time planning their social lives or lying on the couch than they do designing a better life. Distraction and procrastination seek to destroy our ambitions and are often masked in forms such as not having enough time, not having enough money, or any number of other excuses. Regardless of what alibi we offer to justify our circumstances, success requires desire and faith to enter our consciousness, where it mixes with imagination to start an inferno.

Imagination gives life to your desires, but be cognizant that most people give up at the first sign of adversity. If you truly have a burning obsession and you properly understand Hill's principles, you will begin with the end in mind, stopping only when plans require recalibration or when your desire has been transmuted into its physical equivalent. From a young age, record-breaking professional fighter Conor McGregor knew this better than most. "I was just using my imagination," the Irishman said of his against-the-odds success. "It's all I do; it's all I think about."

Your imagination acts on what it has been fed from what you do each day. To harness the full creative spirit, retain the definite purpose as the primary weapon in your arsenal, but spend your time wisely. Through this process, you will inevitably come into contact with the resources, the people, and the inspiration needed to transmute your desire into its physical equivalent.

Barbara Corcoran

At a Catholic elementary school in the blue-collar town of Edgewater, New Jersey, third-graders looked eagerly ahead. While some in the cohort were interested in learning, most were driven by fear. The nuns who ran the classes were notoriously strict and would not tolerate insolence.

In the third row sat Barbara Corcoran, who seemed unusually attentive but could only manage a D average on her report cards. As the second of 10 kids in her family, Corcoran by necessity had quickly mastered the skills of group dynamics and, despite her dyslexia, was determined to keep off Sister Stella Marie's radar. She had fallen foul of the sister many times before, having her ear tugged or neck slapped as punishment and being told that she should change her ways or she would remain stupid forever.

While Corcoran conformed and maintained eye contact as the sister paced, the ways her brain lit up had nothing to do with what was happening in the classroom. Her learning difficulties made it extraordinarily tough to concentrate on school activities or learn anything in this manner, especially for an entire day. So Corcoran multitasked—maintaining the appearance of attention, but giving her brain license to roam, and roam it did. Behind her sparkling blue eyes, the eight-year-old unleashed her imagination, meticulously planning every detail of her life outside the classroom.

⁓⌇⁓

In 1973, Corcoran was waitressing at a diner when the double aluminum doors at the far end opened. The 23-year-old looked up from the table she was scrubbing and toward the enigmatic figure of Ramone Simone. "With his olive skin, jet black hair, and blue aviator shades, he looked nothing like the working-class people who frequented the place," Corcoran recalls.

The pair hit it off and began dating. Property developer Simone—divorced, eight years her senior, and father to three children—asserted that Corcoran would be great in real estate sales and promised to help get her out of the diner and on the pathway to success. A few months later, with a cautionary word from her family, Corcoran plonked her suitcase into the trunk of Simone's yellow Lincoln and climbed onto the leather seat on the passenger side. As the car started toward New York City, she took one last look at the family home and pondered her future.

To get Corcoran settled, Simone paid for a week's accommodation at the Barbizon Hotel for Women. She would have one week to find a job and then an apartment of her own. After an interview for a receptionist position, she was offered a job with the Giffuni Brothers, well-known property landlords who owned more than a dozen buildings in Manhattan and Brooklyn. By week's end, Corcoran had also obtained an apartment and found two other people to share the rent.

Corcoran was a natural people person and reveled in her new role with the Giffuni Brothers. She answered the phones enthusiastically, never called in sick, and earned their trust. It was her first exposure to the property scene. While her skills grew, Simone had plans of his own. He helped get Corcoran set up with a rental real estate company of her own in New York's Upper East Side, taking 51% equity in return for a $1,000 contribution. Corcoran-Simone was born.

With the company set up, all Corcoran needed were actual properties to rent. Ignoring her doubts, she approached one of the Giffuni brothers and asked for a favor—if he could provide her with a single listing, as a reward for the year and a half of service she had rendered. Giffuni agreed, but the listing he offered was a dingy third-floor apartment. "He gave me the worst one," Corcoran remembers. "Maybe it was a challenge, maybe nobody could rent it. Who knows." But one was better than none.

With enough cash for a lone ad in *The New York Times*, Corcoran knew it was sink or swim. She scanned competitor listings to get a feel for what would resonate with prospective tenants and then came up with an idea. Most properties in the city at that time had L-shaped living rooms. The eager property agent asked Giffuni if she could build a half wall with a double entrance to separate the short part of the L from the rest of the living room, promising that she could extract another $40 per month from would-be tenants. He agreed, and Corcoran placed the ad: "One-bedroom apartment with den," which sounded much more enticing than a simple one-bedroom. The phone rang off the hook. It was such a successful formula that the Giffuni Brothers gave Corcoran every one-bedroom apartment they had and built a wall in every one of them.

Corcoran's remuneration was equivalent to the first month's rental, and she had learned a valuable lesson in the process: perception is reality, not the other way around. With her first commission, she visited the luxury department store Bergdorf Goodman and bought a brown-and-white wool herringbone coat, with a big swirly collar and cuffs. "If I looked like I was capable, then I was capable," she said. Word started to spread, and soon other property owners fought to get their listings in front of Corcoran.

In 1977, just a few years after founding Corcoran-Simone, she made her first apartment sale. The New York property scene was in the grip of change, and city governance restrained landlords from asking market rent from tenants. Soon, almost every rental building with a good address in New York City turned into a co-op building.[2]

2 Unlike a traditional apartment where the buyer owns a designated apartment, a co-op allows the buyer to own shares in the corporation that owns the building the apartment is in.

It was the answer to every landlord's dreams: they could cash out of the building and leave the bad tenants behind, a radical change for the region. For the property agents, who put in the same amount of effort to secure a rental as a sale, the co-op commission of 6% of sale price was much more attractive than the one-month rental commission. To capitalize on the change, Corcoran converted her team from rental agents to sales agents as quickly as she could.

While the rental-to-co-op transformation swirled, the 29-year-old's personal life was about to be rocked as well. Five years after they started their business, Simone told Corcoran their relationship was over because he had fallen in love with her secretary. They divided the company's assets and went their separate ways. "You'll never succeed without me," Simone offered as a parting shot. But he was just the latest in a long line of people who seemed to enjoy selling her short. Corcoran smiled through gritted teeth, made a vow that Simone would never see her fail, and got to work building her empire.

Relying on her people skills, Corcoran started building a team of people who all had one attribute in common—when they took a hit, they didn't take long to get back up. Fully in control of a company for the first time, she launched the *Corcoran Report*, a twice-yearly publication that provided an overview of New York City's real estate statistics and trends. She only had data from the 11 sales her company had made that year, but she did not wait until she was ready and certainly did not ask anyone else's permission—she simply acted. While it offered a service that people enjoyed, Corcoran had grander motives. "Reporters depend on statistics for stories," she reasoned. "I figured if I could dole them out, I'd always get quoted. Plus, no one ever bothered to ask how many sales it was based on."

Adjusting to the macroeconomic climate, creating a culture of innovation and competitiveness within her team, and working harder than ever, the Corcoran Group grew into a major player in the New York property scene. It opened a large office on Madison Avenue in one of the most iconic parts of the city and looked well positioned to create a prosperous future for its 35 agents. Times were good, and there was no indication of what was to come.

In October 1987, the stock market crashed—an event now known as Black Monday. Stock prices were decimated, and it created unprecedented volatility in world markets. Interest rates had climbed to over 17%, so people borrowed money only out of sheer necessity. Most importantly, investor fear at the time created a stalemate. The phone stopped ringing as people chose to wait it out.

Corcoran was forced to mortgage her home and obtain a salaried job externally—selling condominiums as a property agent for a new development. She used whatever income she brought in to keep her own business afloat. Because the Corcoran Group was able to ride out, by the slimmest of margins, the negative market sentiment, they were able to reconsolidate and stay alive. It had been a close call, however, and offered another important business lesson for the aspiring property guru. "Every dime I made, I had to think about best use," Corcoran reflects. "It's real money, born out of enormous hard work. That's the kind of money you don't lose so fast."

One unforeseen advantage arose from the devastation, though: it thinned the ranks of her competitors. In 1991, with the business still trying to find its feet again, Corcoran's phone rang—a local property developer, Bernie Mendik, asked for her help in selling more than 250 small apartments situated in a dozen buildings around Manhattan. Upon inspection, Corcoran realized they were small and overpriced, in C-rated buildings, some without kitchens. "They could not be sold in a normal market," she thought. "Only in a desperate market." Corcoran approached Mendik and shared her belief.

"You're smart, Barbara." he replied. "You'll figure it out."

It reminded Corcoran of a conversation she had as a child in the Edgewater home. After dinner one evening, her mother had gently taken her aside to say she'd received a call from Sister Stella Marie. "Sister said you're having trouble reading?" Seven-year-old Corcoran sheepishly nodded, trying to fight back the tears. "Don't worry about it—you have a wonderful imagination," her mother continued. "And with it, you can fill in *any* blanks."

Corcoran pondered Mendik's statement. "He's right," she thought to herself, reflecting on all the success she'd been able to have to that point, despite what other people believed. She gathered her salespeople and told them of her plan—they were going to have a city-wide firesale. The Corcoran Group commoditized the apartments by slashing prices and offering them in tiered categories as part of a special one-day "first in, first served" sales event. By day's end, 101 apartments had been sold, and the Corcoran Group had made more than $1 million in commissions. Four months later, Corcoran phoned Mendik to let him know that all the apartments had been sold.

As the sentiment turned in New York, the Corcoran Group—with a stronger balance sheet—was able to grow quickly, becoming the premier real estate firm in the region. Corcoran cites her ability to recruit and retain world-class staff as one of the cornerstones of her success. From the moment each person started, she would nurture them as she would her own family, creating a distinctly high-performing team working toward their common interests. Leading by example, Corcoran ensured a fiercely competitive streak existed throughout the company, underpinned with a culture of fun. "I'm a meticulous planner of good times," the property guru says. "It takes a lot of good planning, creative thought, attention to detail, an element of surprise, and a leader who's willing to make sure everyone has fun." These good times weren't just to help people unwind: some of the company's best innovations came off the back of these events. Another by-product was that the culture of fun ended up being the best recruiting tool, too.

In 2001, after growing the Corcoran Group to the largest of its type in New York with more than $2 billion in sales volume and 1,000 property agents, Corcoran sold the business for an estimated $70 million. The girl from Edgewater, who had used her imagination to overcome learning difficulties and parlayed lessons from her homemaker mother into a multi-billion-dollar business, had made it.

Today, Barbara Corcoran is more popular than ever as a television personality on the hit series *Shark Tank*. She has invested in more than 30 start-up businesses and enjoys helping entrepreneurs navigate the perilous route to success. In her limited downtime, she most enjoys spending time with husband, Bill, and two children, Tom and Katie.

Corcoran is also deeply passionate about helping people rise above their circumstances, realizing that what people think of *themselves* is far more important than what others think. "My learning difficulties made me more creative, more social, and more competitive," she believes. "What an advantage this so-called weakness was."

Rob Dyrdek

One Sunday afternoon in Dayton, Ohio, after a local skateboard tournament, a young boy followed one of his favorite pros, Neil Blender, out to his limousine. As Blender opened the door, the boy spoke: "Hey, I don't think there's enough room for you and that board."

"You know what? You're right!" Blender said, handing his young fan the skateboard.

Eleven-year-old Rob Dyrdek had learned one of the universe's most valuable lessons, one that many go their whole lives without properly understanding: *Whatever the mind can conceive and believe, it can achieve.*

With his new skateboard, Dyrdek practiced religiously. One year later, his hard work paid off. He was named the youngest ever member of the prestigious G&S skateboarding team.

Dayton had only a small skating community, and Dyrdek's prodigious talent began to attract the attention of more sponsors. After a couple of years, he made the decision to quit high school and focus on the sport he loved. Each morning, Dyrdek would get dropped off to the local skate shop—owned by an ambitious entrepreneur, the 19-year-old Jimmy George—and put in hours of practice to build his skills, before his father picked him up on the way home from work.

Aside from attention to his craft, spending each day at the skate shop gave him a behind-the-scenes look at an actual operating business. The sport exploded in popularity, and soon Dyrdek had a front-seat view of the companies and brands his friends, like George, built in front of him—from idea generation and product design to marketing and operations. It was an education via the real world. Innately curious, Dyrdek looked on, observing how these businesses needed to grow to survive. That period instilled in the young skateboarder an obsession with the relentless pursuit of growth in all aspects.

Following the lead from his friends and early mentors, Dyrdek tested his business acumen on the only thing he could—his own career. When the skills of Dayton's hottest skating prospect translated into financial reward, the 15-year-old tracked every dime that came his way. One year later, he turned pro and moved to California for a shot at the big time.

In the coming years, Dyrdek would get the first opportunity to flex his entrepreneurial spirit, co-founding a company that manufactured "trucks"—the metal axles that hold the wheels. He envisioned the name, created the logo, and designed the product for a brand that struck an instant chord with the emerging culture, at one stage having the world's 10 best ranking skaters on the team.

Dyrdek's profile continued to soar. One of his chief sponsors, California brand Droors Clothing, decided to enter what was then the "blue ocean" of athletic shoes specifically designed for skateboarding. DC approached Dyrdek to see if he wanted to help get their new project off the ground. He agreed, and designed a forward-thinking, innovative, practical shoe, complete with the lace loops that were a staple on popular athletic shoes from other sports.

While happy with his design, Dyrdek wasn't sure if DC—or, more importantly, the consumer market—would share his enthusiasm. Without any formal background in the professional elements of design, he was relying on instinct for his competitive advantage.

But the new footwear project exploded. Given his profile in skateboarding and booming sales, Dyrdek was able to negotiate royalty deals for each pair he played a role in creating. With every design pitch, he drew on showmanship honed from his time dazzling audiences on his skateboard, whipping the sales team into a frenzy with stories of what each design would represent for the culture.

With every successful pitch, the hand-sketched designs would be handed to the DC staff to finalize—to round out the concept, source materials, prepare the tech pack for manufacturing, bring to market, and promote. The design process gave Dyrdek a much-needed creative outlet away from the prying eyes of the public. His work dominated the range, until more than one-third of the line was attributed to his talent. At 23 years old, he had the world at his feet, and his mind raced with ways he could build the Dyrdek empire.

With increasing commitments came a whole lot of pressure. As money poured in to skateboarding, the sport quickly evolved and commercialized, requiring more from its athletes. Sponsors clamored for market share and expected their athletes to play an increasingly important role in growing the brand. At DC, the salaried designers began to resent the influence one skateboarder could have on their company and how much money he could make without even being in the office day to day. Dyrdek's success also led to more opportunities off the board, and he now presided over an empire that had diversified interests across multiple industries. It was the perfect storm. With all these distractions, his passion for skateboarding—and commitment to improving his skills—began to wane.

He was called in for a meeting with DC staff, who tabled him a two-year contract that assumed his professional athletic career would expire at 25: "Rob, we believe your best years are behind you. But there'll always be a spot for you here on the design team."

Feeling dismayed, Dyrdek searched for answers. He questioned his life to that point and tried to figure out who he wanted to be. The search led him to La Jolla, just north of San Diego, where he met with clinical psychologist and peak performance coach Dr. George Pratt. It was far more enlightening than the skateboarder ever thought possible. The sessions with Pratt helped him identify a lack of true purpose and revealed he subconsciously felt he didn't even deserve success. Pratt suggested the sporadic creation of business ventures were attempts to find an ongoing source of passion and energy that would serve as rocket fuel for Dyrdek's seemingly infinite well of ambition. They reframed his situation, developed a plan, and got Dyrdek back on the board with a single aim—to prove his naysayers wrong.

He eliminated all the distractions that had shifted his focus away from mastery of his craft: the unhealthy lifestyle, ad hoc business interests, and reliance on natural talent in place of consistent purposeful practice. Dyrdek also revisited *Think and Grow Rich*, a book he had first read six years prior, and set about turning the success principles into habit.

With his new sense of purpose and renewed passion for the sport, Dyrdek's career rose to new heights. The conversation with DC had been discouraging, but it set up a chain reaction that would catapult his career. The self-awareness he developed through the process showed him what he needed to perform at the highest levels in all aspects of his life—on the skateboard, in an office, and in personal relationships. Most importantly, it taught him to be happy.

A decade on, as his peers began to retire, Dyrdek continued to play an instrumental role in shaping the culture of skateboarding. He went on to have 29 signature model shoes with DC, selling millions of pairs. He evolved his personal brand to success in the mainstream media, creating and starring in three hit television shows before his thirty-sixth birthday: *Rob & Big*, *Fantasy Factory*, and *Ridiculousness*. He also created, produced, and voiced the animated series *Wild Grinders* and has been closely involved in the development of numerous video games.

In 2010, Dyrdek launched the international competitive series Street League Skateboarding. Aside from offering the largest cash prize in the sport's history, the SLS seeks to foster acceptance from mainstream society, helping to solidify skateboarding as a legitimate worldwide sport. The venture worked, and it's now regarded as the premier competitive series in skateboarding and is broadcast on television around the world.

To make the most of his media opportunities, Dyrdek learned everything he could about how to apply the right tactics to this new career for ultimate long-term gains. He realized that controlling the verticals—production, sponsors, and viewing rights—would give him continually greater leverage and considerably more cashflow for every finished product that matched his lofty aspirations. To this day, his media expansion continues at a voracious pace.

For all his success, his crowning glory is the Dyrdek Machine, a venture capital business established in 2016 to accelerate the growth of early-stage companies. Dyrdek spent years putting the Machine in place—drawing on experiences from his own life and partnering with the smartest people he could find—to drive success for the individuals and companies in which he chooses to invest, the purveyors of disruptive companies built to last forever.

"We've engineered the fundamental operational, brand, and financial systems we believe all profitable, sustainable, meaningful companies possess into a science. The art is finding the people and ideas and putting the pieces together," Dyrdek says of his passion project.

For a man who always looked bigger than his circumstances, helping the next generation of entrepreneurs build a roadmap for their own success is a mission in which he takes great pride. Understanding what the business mogul wants in an investment may seem complicated—individuals and companies must illustrate how they fulfill the 99 truths outlined on the Dyrdek Machine website. However, the ones who catch his attention primarily need to fulfill two simple attributes: zest for life and a bulletproof plan.

At 42 years of age, Rob Dyrdek works from a penthouse office in Beverly Hills, with 360-degree views of one of the most glamorous cities in the world. He considers *Think and Grow Rich* an instrumental part of his consistent growth and continues to read it to this day. To maintain harmony in his life, Dyrdek focuses on three things—working on ventures in which he believes, committing to mastery of the business world, and creating a platform of love for his young family.

It's this life plan—what he calls his "rhythm of existence playbook"—that maintains Dyrdek's infinite well of energy and is what he regards as his greatest accomplishment. "It's creating your entire universe about you being at your best, living with energy every day, and just being happy," he offers. "That's the ultimate freedom."

ORGANIZED PLANNING

THE CRYSTALLIZATION OF DESIRE INTO ACTION

"People are not paid for what they know. They are paid for what they do with what they know."
—NAPOLEON HILL

ORGANIZED PLANNING TRANSFERS THE ENERGY OF desire and imagination into its physical equivalent. Any great success has been achieved through the coordinated efforts of many, directed toward a definite purpose.

Do not confuse individual success with individual effort to achieve success, for real success is achieved on the back of faultless plans prepared in cooperation with the experience, education, talents, and imagination of a determined group of people who believe in your end goal. Even the smartest mind cannot ascend to lofty heights without the input and support of others who are committed to their definite purpose. Take careful note: for sustainable harmony and productivity, you must clearly show the people best positioned to aid in your journey the value you will provide to them in return.

Every shortcoming in your life can be attributed to a weak plan for its attainment. Constantly learn from your own experiences and from those around you to craft the finest, most detailed, and most concrete plan you can, with but one condition: do not wait—the time will never be just right. With the right mindset, you will acquire everything you need along the way.

On this journey, you will encounter adversity and temporary defeat. Nothing is more certain. However, if your plan seems futile, replace it with a new plan that will guide you to your burning desire. Use the eighth principle—persistence—to come up with as many organized plans as you need before success is attained, remembering that every doomed plan stems from not being properly prepared in the first place. In your darkest days, find comfort knowing that almost every great fortune was made after paying the price of near ruin.

There are two types of people in this world: leaders and followers. If you wish to be regarded as an authority in your chosen field, you must draw on imagination for creative thought and direct it toward organized plans that attract ongoing prosperity and opportunity into your life. However, when starting out, do not diminish the importance of being a good follower, for it can often be the surest path to being a powerful leader.

Plans crafted alone are like a sail with no hull. Even the wildest imagination is no match for definite, practical plans—carefully prepared in cooperation with your mastermind group—that seek to lead you to victory.

Derek Mills

Derek Mills gasped for air. The shocking news literally took his breath away. "Your mother has died," the family's neighbor repeated. "It's a dream, it's a dream, it's a dream," Mills frantically whispered to himself, programming his brain to block out the pain. The 13-year-old went to bed that night and closed his eyes as quickly as he could, praying that the next morning his mother would be there to give him a hug and tell him everything was all right. But for Mills, his father, and his six siblings, the loss was real. Their lives had changed forever.

The teenager's shock manifested itself in his speech. Returning to school, on the outskirts of Birmingham, England, after the funeral, the teacher asked him to read a passage from a book that was being passed around. As his classmates stared, and after what felt like minutes of fighting for any sound, Mills burst out, "C-c-c-an't s-s-s-s-peak." He sank his head in misery, hearing the muffled laughs and whispers of his peers. As one of the school's few black kids, he was used to feeling like an outcast, but after the tragic loss he withdrew from everyone. The relentless taunts on multiple fronts—but particularly his speech—battered his self-esteem.

The stutter became his companion throughout high school and followed him to college, where he studied engineering. In his second year, Mills dropped out of college, having acquired only one piece of knowledge—that he didn't want to be an engineer. Mills eventually found full-time work as a civil servant for the social services department. Due to his limited education and experience, he was offered the position of clerical officer, the second lowest rank in the entire organization. However, he was satisfied with the steady pay, the relatively cushy government role, and its corresponding pension. But after a year, he was on thin ice with his supervisor, as he continued to make mistakes in his work. "I did so badly at that job," he recalls, "that within 18 months I was the only person in the organization ever to be demoted to clerical assistant."

He moved to the city and obtained a commission-only job as a trainee salesman of life insurance, savings, and pension products. Being more client facing, it would be impossible to mask his speech impediment, but Mills reframed the situation as an advantage, noting that people would need to lean in to him and, as a result, would be paying much closer attention to what he had to say. He managed to close some deals—enough to stay employed.

One day, his boss asked the 25-year-old if he could assist with the recruiting sessions the company was holding that day. "I just need you to speak with the candidates in the next room. Introduce yourself, give an overview of the company, and then welcome me for the presentation," he said. Recoiling in terror, Mills summoned all the courage he could and walked into the room, where he was instantly met with 15 pairs of eyes gazing right at him. As he attempted to address the young professionals, he could feel the sweat break out of every pore in his body. He blurted out a few sentences, the debilitating anxiety magnifying his stutter. After a few agonizing minutes, Mills signaled his boss to enter and retreated to his desk.

A month later, a letter landed on his desk from a woman who had been one of the young professionals interviewed. "Mr. Mills, I applied for a job as a trainee broker at the company you work at, and I didn't get the job," the letter opened. After several references to how strong her candidacy was, her barbs turned to Mills. "You babbled incoherently and no one could understand a word you said. I can't believe I can't get a job with a company where someone who can't even speak properly works." Humiliated, Mills fought back the tears to save face in front of his colleagues. He scrunched up the letter and tossed it away. But then he pondered his situation further—an inner voice whispered that perhaps some good could come from this experience. "The woman who wrote the letter is absolutely right," he thought. "I can't speak properly. But that's all going to change." For the second time in his life, Derek Mills was going to learn to speak.

Every Monday for 14 weeks, Mills attended a speakers' program hosted by Dale Carnegie Training. At the end, his tenacity paid off and he was awarded "most improved" out of his cohort, "although I was coming from a low base!" he laughs. As his speaking skills improved, his zest for life returned. In six years, using mental fortitude and the techniques he was taught in the speakers' program, his stutter had completely disappeared. However, the next battle was about to begin.

By his mid-thirties, despite now having considerable experience in the financial services industry and a more confident demeanor, the bills just seemed to stack up faster and faster. He wanted to be a good provider for his wife, Gerry, and their four children, but struggled to make ends meet. To increase his income, he worked longer hours and would concede to every client request—whether meeting them late at night or traveling several hours for a single appointment. With less time for his family, and still failing to make a dent in the pile of bills, the relationships around him began to erode in line with the mounting stress. Mills's car had 200,000 miles on the odometer and seemed to be perpetually in need of repair. Worse, the harder he tried, the more miserable he became.

One day, while toiling away in the office, the phone rang. "Derek, the bailiffs are in the house," Gerry said, worriedly. "They're not going to take our house today, but they will if we haven't paid the bills within seven days."

Mills bluffed confidence: "Leave it with me, darling. I'll take care of it."

"Okay," Gerry responded. "Do you remember that my parents are visiting from Ireland?"

"Yes, of course."

"Well, they're here now. With the bailiffs."

Mills hung up the phone. "My humiliation was complete at that point," he reflects.

The spiral continued, until a moment in 2003 when the depressed financial adviser—ranked 1,200th in the company for new business revenue—reached a tipping point. Another early start had rolled into another long night. At 9:30 P.M., the security guard warned that he would be locking up soon. "Just give me 10 more minutes," Mills sighed. The 38-year-old sifted through the client folders in the filing cabinet, looking for any opportunities to generate business. The guard approached again. "Two more minutes," Mills pleaded.

"What time did you get in this morning?" the guard asked.

"Well, 8 A.M.," Mills replied.

As the guard shuffled off, a despondent Mills thought, "I've been up since 6 A.M., on the road at 7 A.M., in the office at 8 A.M. It's now almost 10 P.M., and by the time I get home it will be 11 P.M. I've been doing this for years. Away from my family, working all these hours, and having absolutely nothing to show for it." Exasperated, and with as much force as he could muster, he slammed the filing cabinet door.

An inner voice told him, "This is not your life; you're not meant for this. You're not happy because you're not being who you truly are." Mills thought about what a successful life meant for him. In that moment, he realized he needed to set daily standards and live by them, one day at a time. He grabbed a piece of paper and wrote down all the criteria of a successful life as his true self: taking his kids to school each morning, picking them up three days a week, no working on weekends, and focusing on his health by exercising each day. Mills even made rules around his clients: their income, their assets, no evening appointments, no appointments out of his office, and that they had to be nice people. He color-coded each part, outlined them on a large sheet, made several copies, and then laminated each one.

The next day, Mills handed a copy to Gerry and told her she had a new husband. Then he gave a copy to his children and said they had a new dad. He took another copy and stuck it on the refrigerator. These went beyond goals—they were daily standards that, if upheld, would give him everything he ever wanted in life. "Because I made the decision to be that person, I was instantly happier," Mills says. "My happiness was no longer tied to future achievement, but to living my daily standards."

As he settled into his new life, Mills noticed that people began to connect with him more. He removed the 90% of his clients who were the source of most of his frustrations, knowing that he would endure financial hardship in the short-term but having faith that it would all work out over time. Within one year, his income had increased 50%. The following year, it doubled. Then, in 2005, it doubled again. By 2006, Mills was a millionaire—all while staying in the same job and sitting in the same office. Within three years, he was ranked as one of the top performers in his company for new business revenue and was promoted to senior partner. His new outlook increased his income tenfold, all while working less than half the time he had previously.

Supremely confident with his new life, Mills released the bestselling book *The 10-Second Philosophy* to help people discover the true genius hidden within them and began mentoring C-level executives to align success and happiness in their personal and professional lives. Derek Mills continues his work as one of the United Kingdom's leading wealth advisers, only now his mission has a much greater mandate. Today, the motherless boy who was teased because of his speech impediment travels around the world inspiring audiences of all backgrounds with his message of hope. Better yet, Mills is a doting husband and father to his wife, Gerry, and their four children.

In the last 15 years, Derek Mills has proven that listening to your inner voice and committing to daily standards can unlock happiness and prosperity in all areas of life.

Joel Brown

Thump.

Joel Brown felt the fist hit his face, simultaneously cracking and buckling his front teeth. The impact knocked him to the ground.

Only it didn't feel like a fist.

Taking a few seconds to gather his thoughts, he looked up. Standing over him was someone who had taunted him for years. The bully waited for his victim to get up for more. Brown looked at the rage in his eyes, but a glisten shifted his gaze. The sucker punch had been delivered flush to Brown's jaw with brass knuckles.

The following day, recuperating at home, 16-year-old Brown reflected on what had brought him to that point. Only a few years earlier he had seen some of his fellow students—those more academically minded, overweight, or of foreign descent—on the receiving end of regular bullying from schoolyard toughs. Born with a disdain for injustice in any form, Brown had decided to intervene, hoping that it would ease the burden for students whose time at school was a living hell. This made him a target, but he felt confident enough in himself to handle it.

As the years wore on, Brown had become skilled at ignoring the verbal barrages and constant taunts, but this level of violence went beyond what he would tolerate.

Finally, disillusioned with high school, Brown found solace in music. That journey led him to a local radio station where, at 22 years of age, his resourcefulness, love of hip-hop music, and sound knowledge of audio engineering earned him his own radio show. Seeing this as an opportunity to shine, Brown studied everything he could find on internet marketing and promotion to help make his new show a success. The ratings reflected his hustle, and he was shifted to the prime-time slot.

More motivated than ever, Brown reached out to major labels in the United States—Atlantic, Sony, and Capitol Records—and was able to speak directly to representatives of some of the highest profile hip-hop artists, and occasionally the artists themselves.

Two DJs who worked at Brown's radio station were into producing their own music. Seeing an opportunity for growth, Brown asked, "If I can get your beats into the hands of these artists in the United States and they then use them on a track, can I get a cut of the profits?" They agreed. Overnight Joel Brown had become a manager in the music industry.

With the same drive and fearlessness that had spawned his previous successes, he spoke with his contacts in the United States and emailed them some beats in which they might be interested. Eventually, their music made it into the hands of platinum hip-hop artist T-Pain and his 12-time Grammy-award-winning producer. On behalf of his artists, Brown signed a publishing deal with

Rebel Rock—a division of Atlantic Records—and flew to Miami for a two-year stint in the epicenter of a thriving hip-hop industry.

While it was a dream for Brown, there was more to the industry than the on-camera glitz. The bureaucracy of a major corporation meant layers of approval and hoops to jump through. Brown longed for the freedom to act on intuition, and his entrepreneurial spirit swelled. Something was missing. A passage from a book he read as a child had looped through his head for years: *You don't have to work for money, you can make money work for you.*

On a whim, Brown said goodbye to the music industry and booked a ticket home to Perth, Australia, a world away from the excitement of Miami. The plane landed in San Francisco at midnight, but a late departure meant he missed the connecting flight. Lying in his hotel room, a frenzy of scenarios and doubts ran through his head. Suddenly a booming voice came through the television: "You've got to follow your passion! Never settle." The voice belonged to self-help legend Anthony Robbins. To Brown, it felt like a sign from the universe that he had made the right choice.

Back in Perth, he got his hands on every personal development book he could find, from Napoleon Hill to Jack Canfield, and everything in between. The day after he landed, a sales company offered him a role selling telecommunication solutions. Brown knew this was not what he wanted to do, but he resolved to do the best he could at it while he figured out what he did want to do.

His reading had equipped him with the know-how to implement sales tactics with dramatic effect. Nine months later, as one of the company's top sellers, he was invited to a private sales training event with Jordan Belfort, author of *The Wolf of Wall Street*, who was doing a seminar tour before the release of the Scorsese film on his life. Belfort had a colorful past, but he was on a mission to turn his life around by teaching people how to sell ethically.

Belfort called for a volunteer to work with him in front of the group, and Brown stepped up. Belfort got in his face and asked him to write down three things:

- What are you good at?

- What do you love?

- What solution are you bringing to the world?

It was the first time since high school that Brown had been asked to put pen to paper, and he still bore a distaste for it. Belfort insisted, saying: "Between those things is the most important intersect you could imagine: purpose. Build that purpose into your subconscious and the universe will get out of your way to make it happen."

Brown answered those questions, then wrote out a 10-year plan that contained everything he ever wanted— the craziest desires he could concoct. Then he reverse engineered it, writing down what he would need to achieve in year nine to hit that 10-year goal, then year eight, right back to year one.

For the first time in his life, Joel Brown knew exactly what he wanted. Better yet, he had a detailed blueprint to get there.

He committed to building a website, *Addicted2Success*, that would fight injustice on a much greater scale, allowing people around the world to ignore the negative pull around them and live the life of their dreams.

Brown noted his metric for success as 10 million views, which he hoped to achieve by the 10-year mark, an exceptionally audacious goal for a website that didn't yet exist.

To get started, he took a job that would provide him with a larger and more reliable income to get his new project off the ground: he moved to the Western Australian desert, where he helped relocate animals that were in the way of large-scale construction projects. It was a tough life, working 12-hour shifts in 115-degree heat (46 degrees Celsius) and sleeping in makeshift cabins in one of the most remote locations in the world.

Almost everyone in the camp talked incessantly about how much they hated life and how bad they had it. To avoid their negative energy and fixed mindsets, Brown would sit in his car and listen to audio recordings from his favorite personal development leaders. After his shift, he would work on the *Addicted2Success* website, eventually launching and attracting visitors from around the world.

Fifteen months later, with the steady growth of website traffic and advertising revenue, Brown approached his boss: "It's costing me too much to be here. I'm out." As he left the camp, the 25-year-old made a promise to himself: he would never work a 9–5 job again.

Five years into the *Addicted2Success* journey, Joel Brown has achieved all but one of the goals on his 10-year plan—to speak on the same stage as Anthony Robbins. He is scheduled to fulfill that goal in a few months' time. Today, Brown hosts a podcast with over a million listens and commands a social media audience of two million people, and his website has had more than 100 million unique views.

In 2016, in association with Pencils of Promise, he built a school in Laos to help children living in poverty.[3] Aside from offering resources and educational materials most lacking in the region, the school teaches children that the world is how they view it—that their success is intrinsically linked to their imagination.

With Joel Brown's relentless focus, he achieved his 10-year vision in half that time.

---

3 Pencils of Promise is a non-profit organization that builds schools and increases educational opportunities in the developing world.

DECISION
The mastery of procrastination

"Tell the world what you intend to do.
But, first, show it."
—Napoleon Hill

IN THE ORIGINAL *THINK AND GROW RICH*, HILL noted that the 500 successful people he interviewed firsthand reached decisions promptly and changed their decisions slowly. Indeed, an overarching theme of success throughout the ages is decisively hammering a stake into the ground, declaring your intent to the universe, and then defending it at all costs.

Proper understanding of decision can also be found by looking at its opposite: procrastination. Test your decision-making abilities by observing your actions in response to reading each chapter of this book. Are you actively channeling the information to creative effect—undertaking immediate, tangible action toward a definite purpose?

Early in her career, billionaire Oprah Winfrey was unceremoniously dumped from her role as television news anchor. Refusing to let the failure define her, Winfrey hammered her stake in the ground and stayed in the media industry. As the years wore on, she developed her skills and was eventually given her own program. *The Oprah Winfrey Show* ran for 25 seasons and remains the highest-rated talk show in American history. "It doesn't matter who you are or where you come from," Winfrey believes, "the ability to triumph begins with you, always."

Had she listened to the advice of executives early on that she wasn't fit for television and cast her dreams aside, the world would have missed out on one of the greatest philanthropists of our time.

Only you can determine how the counsel of those closest to you can help or hinder your mission, but be very careful with the priority you place on different sources of opinion. Give first precedence to your inner voice because you are the only one who can truly and completely lead your burning desire through to reality. Second, heed the wisdom of a well-comprised mastermind group who can multiply your abilities and influence. The healthy counsel of these two sources cannot be overstated.

It is also vital to decide whom not to listen to. There will always be people trying to force their negative, or simply mindless, opinions on you. You must ignore them. Those readily moved by the opinions of others have no desire of their own. Decide what *you* want, then make it happen.

James Hill

James Hill felt adrift. His adolescence had been a mad dash for adulthood—he quickly sought independence so he could enjoy the freedom of making his own decisions. The only catch, as he found out, was that he had to live with the consequences of those decisions.

With limited career prospects, he was drafted into the Marine Corps at the age of 21. It turned out to be a big improvement on his previous low-skill, low-pay jobs. Being a few years older than his peers meant they instinctively viewed him as a leader. This attitude, coupled with a strong work ethic and being tenaciously competitive, allowed Hill to be meritoriously promoted repeatedly, making sergeant at age 23. But while his tenure at the Marine Corps was enjoyable, Hill longed for direction in his personal life—for purpose.

All his life, he had overheard conversations about his famous grandfather, Napoleon, who apparently had made more millionaires than anyone else in history, but he had never grasped how big an achievement that was. Despite exchanging letters during his childhood, his last in-person encounter with his grandfather before he passed had been in his early teens, when Napoleon gifted him a copy of *Think and Grow Rich*, signed in emerald ink on the inside cover. Before he could grab it, the author—through his trademark spectacles—had looked him in the eye, and said the book came with just one condition: "Promise me you'll read it," Napoleon said. "Read it carefully and you can have anything you desire." The memory was so vivid, but James Hill recalled that at the time he'd been more interested in the ten-dollar bill that served as its bookmark. He couldn't help but wonder what Napoleon would think of his wayward grandson today.

Miserable, he found his counterpart in an equally unhappy woman, and they began dating. Lamenting their circumstances—they had no money, no education, and had lost touch with their families—Hill mentioned that his grandfather had seemed to be attuned to a proven formula for success. He lent her the original *Think and Grow Rich*, the one that had been given to him by the author himself, but the pair broke up weeks later. He would never retrieve the book.

The next Friday evening, a despondent Hill wandered into the local supermarket in Beaufort, South Carolina. He grabbed a box of beer—the weekend's entertainment—and stood at the checkout. As he waited his turn to pay, something caught his eye. Right in front of him on the shelf was a stack of *Think and Grow Rich* books, for sale at arm's length from where he stood. The iconic cover brought back a flood of memories: the letters he had written to his grandfather as a boy, the day he had been given the signed copy of the book, and finally remorse as he reflected on how careless he'd been with his original copy. "Time to make amends," Hill thought as he plucked the book from the supermarket shelf.

The 23-year-old stayed home that night, determined to read the whole book front to back. While he enjoyed the read and doggedly underlined any passages that struck a chord, he failed to unearth any great secret that would instantly change his life. Feeling that he surely must have missed something, Hill re-read it the next day.

Working his way through the text again, he came to a passage that caught his attention:

> *No alibi will save you from accepting the responsibility if you now fail or refuse to demand riches of life, because the acceptance calls for but one thing—incidentally, the only thing you can control—and that is a STATE OF MIND. A state of mind is something that one assumes. It cannot be purchased, it must be created.*

As he continued, Hill realized he fell short in other areas too. "Definite purpose? Burning desire? Heck, I didn't even have a goal," he reflects on his mindset at the time.

As he read through each of the "57 Famous Alibis," Hill saw the exact phrases he had uttered for years. He realized that these excuses to justify his mediocrity weren't valid, when most of the achievements that shaped the world in which he lived had been created by those with far, far fewer resources at their disposal and just one extremely powerful weapon in their arsenal—the ability to control their thoughts.

"When I read *Think and Grow Rich* for the second time, I realized that I already had the recipe for success," Hill observed. "It was the key to everything—financial security, personal relationships, happiness—it could be used to achieve anything of value. It could be done by anybody, and it could be done by me. There was just one catch: it was up to me."

Committing to change, he grabbed a notepad and wrote that if he wanted a life of which he could be proud, he had to accept it on faith and dedicate himself to it. He made a list of everything he ever wanted, regardless of how fantastical. His eclectic list was heavily influenced by the science fiction novels he had immersed himself in as a child, including pursuits such as astronaut, doctor, pilot, astrophysicist, policeman, cowboy, and finally, to finish his education. Scanning the list, he noticed that some weren't possible given his circumstances—he removed "astronaut" because he did not have the education or training, then ruled out "doctor" because he did not have the education or the money for medical school.

With most of his list crossed out, he stared at the one item for which he couldn't make an excuse—to finish his education. "I did not know if this was right or not," Hill said. "But at least it was a decision to do something. If you cannot make a decision to do something, you will never make a decision to do anything."

The thought made the hair stand up on the back of his neck. He flipped the notepad over, outlined a plan to make it happen, and then excitedly put it into action— simply embarking on the mission gave him the purpose he craved. College was going to cost money, so Hill figured he would need a scholarship from the Marine Corps. He searched and discovered this might be possible for him via the Navy Enlisted Scientific Educational Program. To receive the scholarship, he would need to perform strongly on the college scholastic aptitude test, and he gave himself one year to make it happen.

A practice test revealed deficiencies in his academic performance. To strengthen his candidacy, he took courses on algebra and trigonometry at a community college, as well as a non-laboratory chemistry course via correspondence. When not on duty as a Marine, he was studying. Anything that did not help him achieve his goal he steadfastly avoided.

When he finally took the SAT, his grades had sky-rocketed—his hard work and discipline had paid off. The Marine Corps awarded him a full scholarship, and in 1974, James Hill was enrolled in engineering at Vanderbilt University, one of the top schools in the country, on full pay and allowances. Better yet, his colonel spoke with Hill's professors about stacking the young Marine's course load, allowing him to finish six months ahead of his peers. In 1978, he had accomplished his goal to finish his education, graduating as one of the top students in his class.

But he wasn't done yet. Hill applied for pilot training in Pensacola, Florida, with the Navy. At 30 years old, he was much older than the typical applicant, but he was given an age waiver and accepted. His examinations on aptitude and spatial relations were excellent, and he was recommended to fly jets. However, to excel as a pilot, he would need to be in the top 1% for multitasking: capable of communicating across various frequencies, monitoring the altimeter, using the rudder to balance each of the wings, keeping the nose of the plane steady, and many more responsibilities—all at the same time.

Hill began his attempt to disconnect mind from body in order to fullfil these tasks. "I would go into my garage with a basketball and run around the chair, bouncing the basketball—or go for a five-mile run with a tennis or golf ball, catching it repeatedly, all while reciting my procedure."

During his pilot training, he received a call saying that each branch of the Armed Forces was to put forward two people who would be trained as mission specialists for the Space Shuttle Program—Hill was asked to represent the Marine Corps. In six years, he had gone from being adrift to completing his engineering degree, flying planes and helicopters, and being considered for a mission in outer space.[4] Remarkably, all were listed on his wish list of what he wanted to accomplish in life.

After his pilot training and some candid introspection, Hill felt he did not have the abilities to truly excel in the new career and resumed his duties with the Marine Corps. However, the six-year journey had been the most remarkable phase of his life and helped him understand that true failure comes only from not trying.

In 1995, Hill was stationed in Hawaii as a battalion executive officer, responsible for 800 Marines. With 26 years of service under his belt, he again found himself at a crossroads—would he accept one last posting in Okinawa, Japan, or retire? Hill attended a cocktail party, where a doctor asked, "What did you want to be before you were in the Marines?"

"Believe it or not, doc, I actually wanted to be a doctor!" Hill responded.

"Well, you still can."

"What do you mean?"

"There are laws against age discrimination," the man continued. "There was a woman in her fifties in my residency program. If you want to go into medicine, you still can."

---

4 The Space Shuttle Program was eventually shelved, but Hill was honored even to be considered for something that six years earlier had been a pipe dream.

Applying for medical school at 47 years old seemed ludicrous to Hill, but he gave it some thought. He wrote letters to five universities, mentioning that he was academically competitive and asking for an honest assessment of his candidacy given his age and background. One replied, urging him to apply, citing that medical students with prior military experience have a discipline that allows them to be good doctors. He sat down with his wife, Nancy, and mulled over the decision.

A few months later, he was accepted into medical school at West Virginia University. As he had done before, he outlined a plan for how he would make it work and set about executing it. And as with his original list so many years earlier, the hair stood up on the back of his neck when he made the decision to take action. In 2001, he graduated from medical school, aged 53.

While having very little by way of a real relationship with his grandfather, James Hill was able to completely transcend his circumstances using Napoleon's wisdom, which served as a guiding star when he needed it most. "The book...it changed everything for me," he says. "It changed my life."

Today, Dr. James Hill is living out his childhood dream as a physician with the Department of Veteran Affairs. He and Nancy adopted two children, a decision inspired by a rotation in pediatrics during the medical program. Hill also hasn't given up on his quest to make it to outer space.

John Lee Dumas

Twenty-two-year-old John Lee Dumas checked his bag to make sure he had the proper textbooks for the day, slung the backpack over his shoulder, and walked out of his dorm room. It was just another Tuesday at Providence College in Rhode Island.

College was a big step outside his comfort zone. He'd grown up in a sleepy country town in Maine, then just prior to graduating high school, he applied for—and was awarded—a Reserve Officers Training Course scholarship. It would cover the full cost of his college tuition and provide a stipend for regular living expenses, while training him as a cadet in the US Army. Dumas hoped this path would allow him to study, travel, make a difference to the world, and still get the right foundation for a thriving corporate career.

The college environment exposed him to diversity and intellectual stimulation that he'd never experienced before. The military discipline, sunrise workouts in particular, were a shock to his system. Despite his chosen path, it was still college, so there were regular parties to break up the drudgery of his grueling schedule.

As he walked past a friend's room, he was called in—all eyes were glued to a television screen showing a picturesque view of the Manhattan skyline. The camera panned, showing thick, billowing smoke shrouding the blue sky. It was Tuesday, September 11, 2001—a day he would never forget.

That evening, President George W. Bush addressed the people. "Our military is powerful, and it's prepared," he asserted. As Dumas stared at the television, he had little doubt that the United States would mobilize to exact justice on the perpetrators of the deadliest terrorist act in history.

In the following days, a heightened sense of urgency filled Dumas's officer training. While most recent graduates had fulfilled their college study and subsequent military commitments without setting foot on a live battleground, these Providence College cadets knew their expertise would be put to the test. Suddenly, they took their training a lot more seriously—their lives would depend on it. Dumas and his classmates graduated as the first commissioned officers since the September 11 attack.

One year later, Dumas was deployed to Iraq with the mission of liberating its oppressed people. Iraq had a long history of conflict, creating a power vacuum and immense danger for anyone on the ground. As a platoon leader in the US Army, the 23-year-old was responsible for 16 men and 4 tanks, a sharp deviation from other college graduates his age who were starting their white-collar careers.

During the 13-month tour, the young American witnessed atrocities beyond comprehension. For the typically jovial Dumas, it was a deeply testing time. In four separate incidents, men from his platoon were killed in action; each burial shook him to the core. "I stared down at my soldiers who were never going to be given the opportunity to live out their lives," he recalls. "It's something I'll never forget."

During his tour of duty, John Lee Dumas committed to two principles that would shape his future: first, he would never take his life for granted; and second, he would never settle for anything less than he was capable of.

Returning to home soil, Dumas continued his military service until the completion of his four-year contract. Due to the ROTC scholarship and his time as an active duty officer, he had no student loans to pay and was financially independent. But he needed to recalibrate mentally, so Dumas took a year off to backpack and trek throughout the world.

At 27 years of age, he felt strong social pressure to obtain a traditional job. If he wanted professional success, there were four main options: law, finance, property, or medicine. He enrolled in law school but quit after one semester—something just didn't feel right. So Dumas moved to Boston, where he was able to secure a job in corporate finance, but again never felt he belonged. One day, he hopped in his car and drove from the East Coast to San Diego in search of opportunity.

Dumas enjoyed the freedom of anonymity in his new Californian surroundings and focused on becoming a success in real estate. He tried his hand at residential property, and then commercial, but the familiar dark feelings emerged. While his environment had changed, not much else had.

Despite a six-year struggle across four cities to find a career path he could grow with, nothing ignited his passion. He wanted to add value to the world, but he simply wasn't *inspired*. At 32 years of age, the former army officer felt totally worthless.

Dumas immersed himself in books, which he hoped would guide him through the difficult period. He searched the internet for three main lists—the world's best self-help books, the world's best business books, and the world's most inspirational books—keeping a note of the titles that overlapped all three lists, and ordered them online. With no consistent employment his finances were tight, so where possible he ordered pre-owned copies. Boxes arrived, full of battered and highlighted books, and he dove in. His personal development journey had begun.

They were dark days, but the books helped him realize that perhaps he could thrive outside a traditional career, that maybe he didn't need to "suck it up" and do what everyone else was doing. During this critical time he began to understand a few things that would be imperative: he was bound only by his imagination; if he wanted success on his terms, he would have to truly believe it would eventually happen for him; and he would need a detailed plan to bring it all together.

The fuse was lit. With every anecdote he read, he wanted to learn more about the achievements of unlikely characters—people who had found success on roads less traveled. He started listening to audiobooks while driving and running so he could devour more and more content. Then as his book expenses mounted, he began searching for equivalent-quality content available at a lower cost. He found podcasts, a downloadable form of audio content that he could play from his computer or mobile device, which were becoming popular free offerings from many producers and business leaders. During any free time, he would listen to as many podcasts as he could. Finally, Dumas started to feel excited, positive, and, most importantly, in control of his future.

In 2012, he searched the burgeoning podcast catalogue for a daily show that shared the stories of successful entrepreneurs. Many came out weekly, fortnightly, or monthly, but there was nothing that came out seven days a week. "Perhaps I should be the one to create it," Dumas thought. "If I want it, surely someone else does, too."

At that stage, the aspiring entrepreneur had no podcast hosting experience whatsoever. From the books he read, Dumas knew how important the influence of other people would be on this journey. He set out to find two people who were in the position he hoped to get to— successful business podcast hosts. He contacted Jaime Masters of the *Eventual Millionaire* and Cliff Ravenscraft of *Podcast Mastermind*, asking if they could mentor him.

They agreed, and despite the high cost, it ended up being one of the best investments Dumas ever made. Hiring experts in this area as his personal coaches quickly filled the information gap and gave his new venture the best possible chance of success.

While his upskilling process continued, Dumas sought a name—one that would resonate with his target market and inspire him to loftier heights. He knew the podcast would be a daily show that interviewed business leaders, so "entrepreneur" had to be in there. A catchy name was also important, but it needed to be of substance—something clearly outlining what the show was about.

One night while listening to *Sports Center*, he heard the announcer say, "Lebron James for three. He's on fire!" John Lee Dumas had his name: *Entrepreneur on Fire* was born.

The next piece of the puzzle was tracking down reputable guests to interview on the show. His mentor, Masters, took him along to a conference at which she was speaking, and introduced Dumas to a host of authorities in the business world.

To be a success, he needed a detailed plan, so he went to work mapping out what the first 40 days would look like. Dumas interviewed lower-profile guests to build confidence in his new craft. With some experience under his belt, he went after the bigger fish.

Via Masters's introductions at the conference, first contact had already been made with many of those whom he wanted to interview. He reasoned that a future email wouldn't be a completely cold lead, and perhaps he might get one or two of the big names to participate. Sure enough, people responded favorably, with many doing it as part of a promotional round for a new book, product, or business they were launching.

Once the first 40 shows were recorded, most simply done over Skype, he rearranged the order to launch with the most impact. On August 15, 2012, his scheduled launch date, Dumas woke up terrified and paralyzed with self-doubt. "Who am I to launch this podcast?" he pondered. "Nobody's going to listen. A daily show will never work."

Five weeks passed, and the recordings sat dormant on a hard drive. Dumas justified the delays as wanting to launch when everything was perfect. Finally, the phone rang. "I'll fire *you* if you don't launch your podcast today," Jaime Masters proclaimed. That morning, the 32-year-old former army officer from Maine launched *Entrepreneur on Fire.*

The first 90 days included an eclectic mix of entrepreneurs and business icons, including Seth Godin, Tim Ferriss, Gary Vaynerchuk, and Barbara Corcoran. With each guest, his skills grew.

Within four years, Dumas released 1,600 episodes of his daily show, accruing more than 44 million listens, all from a simple mission—to deliver free, valuable, and consistent content. In that time, the *Entrepreneur on Fire* brand generated more than $10 million in revenue and spawned other successful ventures.[5] As his audience grew, Dumas would ask about their pain points and what they were struggling with. He was then able to create and deliver products that served his audience and enabled them to take their own businesses to the next level.

In 2013, he created *Podcasters' Paradise*, now regarded as the leading podcast community in the world. Dumas uses it as a platform to teach its 3,000 members how to create, grow, and monetize their own podcast. To date, this project alone has generated more than $4 million in revenue. He has also used crowdfunding websites to launch journals that show his audience how to get out of their comfort zones and take the first steps to achieving the life of their dreams.

Every misstep brought Dumas closer to his purpose, and he now spends his days encouraging people, regardless of their age or other perceived limitation, to change their circumstances to something they're passionate about. "I was anything but an entrepreneur for the first 32 years of my life," Dumas said. "Now I literally am the 'entrepreneur on fire.' It doesn't have to be something you were born with—you can take control at any point."

---

5   Since its launch in 2012, the *Entrepreneur on Fire* monthly income reports have been made available online as an educational tool to help aspiring entrepreneurs gain a true understanding of how the business is performing, including its successes and failures: http://eofire.com/income.

PERSISTENCE
THE SUSTAINED EFFORT
NECESSARY TO INDUCE FAITH

"Riches do not respond to wishes.
They respond to definite plans,
backed by definite desires,
through constant persistence."
—NAPOLEON HILL

SIMPLY CONTINUING IS ONE OF THE SUREST PATHS TO success, just as quitting is one of the surest paths to permanent defeat. Winners look for any reason to advance and in doing so bring themselves ever closer to glory.

An excerpt from the ethos of one of the world's preeminent special forces teams, the US Navy SEALs, embodies the principle of persistence: "If knocked down, I will get back up, every time. I will draw on every remaining ounce of strength to protect my teammates and to accomplish our mission. I am never out of the fight." On the battlefield—where stakes are highest—well-constructed plans are carried out by people obsessed with mission success who refuse to give in, no matter what circumstances arise.

The starting point of all achievement is desire, but it is the *intensity* of desire that determines persistence. An honest self-audit will show your level of persistence, and any shortfalls must be overcome by stoking the flame of desire; every principle and anecdote in this book offers both clues and tangible strategies on how to do this. Pay close attention to your physical and mental health, too. If you are not feeling a sense of achievement at the end of each day, perhaps you need healthier food, better sleep, more exercise, better use of your time, more positive friends, or to eliminate distractions that chip away at your energy. There are no valid excuses for permanent defeat.

Spanx founder Sara Blakely once drove to North Carolina to find a manufacturer for her unique shapewear garment. The 29-year-old visited numerous hosiery mills to explain her idea and see if they could help make it, but she was continually turned away. Blakely persisted, spending the rest of the week meeting with as many manufacturers as she could. The mission appeared to be a failure, and she returned home to come up with a different plan to make her dream a reality. Two weeks later, one of the mill owners phoned to say he had shown the concept to his three daughters who had raved about it. A single idea, backed with persistence, made Blakely the youngest self-made female billionaire in the world.

Remember, poverty consciousness will voluntarily seize the mind that is not occupied with wealth consciousness. Champions in any industry know this and give themselves the best opportunity to win. They persist, even if temporary failure requires plans to be recalibrated—they do not quit. Through this principle, temporary failure is forged into long-term victory.

Warren Moon

"Moon…you *stink!*" the head coach barked.

The 11-year-old was upset enough with himself for throwing the intercepted pass. But this blasting from his coach—in front of the whole team—felt unwarranted and lashed his pride. Tears welled up in his eyes as he slunk off the Baldwin Hills field. But with a few deep breaths, Warren Moon soon composed himself. With steely resolve, the boy swore that he would prove just how great he was.

He'd had a difficult upbringing in Los Angeles during the 1960s. At seven years of age, Moon lost his father to liver disease related to alcoholism, leaving his mother, Pat, to care for Moon and his five sisters in their modest home. As a mother of six, Pat had always worked hard, but adjusting to single parenthood brought on a whole new urgency. She would work during the day, then attend school at night to study nursing. Meanwhile, to keep her children engaged with male mentors, Pat enrolled them in junior sports programs. Pat's dedication to study paid off, and she found a new job as a private duty nurse, taking whatever shifts came her way to help provide for her family. "No matter what was going on, we never felt poor," Moon recalls. "Somehow, she was able to provide for us…through all of that."

Her never-give-up attitude in the face of adversity, coupled with her strong work ethic, rubbed off on Moon, who applied those attributes to his sports. He had taken an instant liking to both basketball and football, but it was the latter that soon became his dream. When he returned home from school, Moon would grab the ball and throw to his friend, Hector, even as the sun set and the streetlights illuminated their makeshift field. Only a stern holler from his mother could stop the aspiring football star from abandoning his practice. When not throwing a football, Moon completed his schoolwork and helped with the household chores. By the age of 11, his dream was to play quarterback in the NFL, and he continued to participate in any football-related activity he could, whether street football, a flag game, or simply target practice to improve his delivery. As he grew older, that dream became an organized plan to make it happen, underpinned by a burning desire to take care of his mother and sisters.

Through his teen years, Moon's superior skills, tireless work ethic, and unwavering self-belief helped him overcome whatever opposition he faced. Word started to spread about the kid with the rocket arm who could throw accurately at 80 yards. However, to his dismay, in his sophomore year at Alexander Hamilton High School, he was regarded as a third-string quarterback, his coach suggesting Moon might find more opportunities if he took up a different position. He would only be brought into the game when the team was well behind on the scoreboard or if there were just minutes left on the clock. Despite the favoritism shown to others, Moon continued to put everything he had into his dream—always first to arrive to training and last to leave—and refused to budge from the quarterback position. Moon was committed to being the best quarterback he could be.

The following year, when Moon was training on the field, varsity coach Jack Epstein approached him. "Young man, I've been watching you," he said. "I like your work ethic, your athleticism, and your demeanor. You're going to be my varsity starting quarterback next year." Moon was surprised, and thrilled—determined to show that Epstein's faith and confidence in him was warranted. Throughout the spring and into the summer he trained harder than ever. The team went on to win the league championship, with Moon named Player of the Year in their conference.

The prodigious football talent began to attract interest from colleges throughout the country; however, all wanted him to switch position—and this was non-negotiable in Moon's eyes. He declined and went on to junior college instead. After a season with West Los Angeles College, where he set school records in his freshman season of 1974, he signed with the University of Washington, primarily because the team allowed him to play his preferred position, at a time when African American quarterbacks in reputable college teams were virtually unheard of. As each obstacle to his aspirations reared its head, Moon would cut it down, taking pride in erasing the chatter from people who felt the game and its players should toe a certain line. "That was my full focus," Moon reflects, "to play well enough that people saw past the color, where I was just a quarterback."

Paired with Don James, a new coach at the University of Washington, both men had a point to prove. In the early days, they faced strong criticism as the losses mounted, but the coach stood firmly alongside his quarterback—especially when much of the abuse turned racial. Coach James also acted as a powerful mentor to Moon, teaching the young football player how goal setting, both on and off the field, could lead to success. Eventually, the team built a synergy, then began to notch up back-to-back wins. Finally, in 1978, the Huskies made it to the Rose Bowl, where they scored an unlikely win against the heavily favored Michigan Wolverines, and Moon received the Most Valuable Player award. Victory silenced the harshest of critics and put the University of Washington on the map. Moon was content in triumph, but for James it was the first of 16 straight winning seasons, including three more Rose Bowl victories.

Despite his growing list of accolades, NFL scouts still speculated that Moon was not athletic enough and that his arm was not strong enough. The premier football player in one of the best conferences in the college system was left in the cold—not a single NFL team was willing to draft him as quarterback. "I was bitter," Moon remembers. "I'd done all I could, proved I belonged at that level, and my own country didn't want me." But he refused to give in by switching positions. Instead, without waiting for the official disappointment in the draft, Moon headed north and signed with the Edmonton Eskimos in the Canadian Football League, in the city known as the "City of Champions."

In his six seasons in the CFL, the determined quarterback led the Eskimos to a record five consecutive Grey Cup league championships, where he also became the first professional quarterback to pass for 5,000 yards in a single season, scooping up numerous awards along the way. Moon's greatness was solidified in 2001 when he was inducted into the CFL Hall of Fame. Of the experience, Moon said, "They gave me a chance to play professional football when they saw something in me that my own country didn't see. I'll always be indebted to the Canadian people for it."

With his stock at an all-time high, Moon began to entertain hopes of a return to his home country to secure a contract with the NFL. In 1984, Moon was signed to the Houston Oilers as quarterback. In his first season with the Oilers, Moon repaid the faith shown to him by the team, throwing for a club record of 3,338 yards. Before his arrival, the Oilers had been struggling to win games consistently. Even with Moon's contributions, the team was on the receiving end of taunts from fans, with much of the abuse now having a racial undertone and directed at Moon personally. Blocking out the distraction, and continuing to focus on being the best quarterback he could be, Moon continued a stellar run of form, and the team was nipping at the heels of the play-offs. He also offered his services to the community in Houston, with a particular passion for helping underprivileged children use sports as a catalyst to achieving success in all areas of their lives. Before the start of the 1989 season, he was given a five-year, $10 million contract extension, setting a record as the highest paid player in the NFL at the time. His persistence had paid off.

Moon continued to break records. In 1990, he led the NFL in passing yards, pass attempts, pass completions and touchdowns, as well as tying Dan Marino's record of nine 300-yard games in a single season. After a successful stint at the Oilers, where he set a franchise record for wins, passing yards, pass attempts, pass completions, and touchdowns, the 34-year-old was traded to the Minnesota Vikings. Approaching an age at which, for many, the body struggles to match the mind's alertness and ambitions—especially in a league as rigorous and demanding as American football—Moon continued to rise. By the time the buzzer sounded on his 17-year NFL career, he had been of service to the Oilers, Vikings, Seahawks, and Chiefs, retiring at 44 years old. His time in the NFL had been a tremendous success, a fitting cherry on top of his five-year post-collegiate career in Canada.

In addition to nine Pro Bowl selections and retiring with the third most passing yards and fourth most touchdown passes in NFL history, Moon's legacy was immortalized in 2006 when he was elected into the Pro Football Hall of Fame in his first year of eligibility. He was the first undrafted quarterback and first African American quarterback to be so honored. To this day, Warren Moon is the only player to be inducted into both the Pro Football Hall of Fame and the Canadian Football Hall of Fame.

Driven by his passion for helping others, the football superstar leads the Crescent Moon Foundation, established in 1989 to award scholarships to underprivileged high school children who demonstrate academic success, involvement in their community, and financial need. It is Moon's hope that recipients of this scholarship can go on to college, unlock their potential, and make a positive impact in their communities. Further, Moon was able to parlay an exceptional on-field career into a powerful brand off the field, with roles as an NFL commentator, mentor to many of the game's promising youngsters, and working alongside sports super-agent, Leigh Steinberg. In 2009, he released the bestselling book *Never Give Up on Your Dream*, a firsthand account of his remarkable journey. "There is no easy path to success," he says. "Everyone faces obstacles. But it's what you do when you get knocked down—that's what makes all the difference."

In 2010, Moon launched Sports 1 Marketing with close friend and business partner David Meltzer to bring awareness and much-needed funds to a variety of causes around the world. In his limited spare time, Moon sits on the board of several non-profit organizations, including St. Jude Children's Research Hospital and the Rose Bowl Foundation.

Warren Moon, who paired an extraordinary work ethic with unwavering self-belief, both qualities inspired by his mother in their family's darkest days, always moved forward regardless of what life threw his way. "I could have listened to what everyone said and changed positions," Moon says, "but quarterback was my dream. And nothing was going to stand in my way."

Brandon T. Adams

"*S, s, s, s...*"

Brandon Adams stared at himself in the mirror. Born with a speech impediment that deeply affected his confidence, he would stand in the same spot every night for purposeful practice. With each careful pronunciation of the letter that gave him the most trouble, he hoped to overcome the lisp that made him a popular victim for bullies. Each schoolyard taunt strengthened the boy's resolve to achieve his goal, but the bullies would feed off any insecurity they could find. The only problem was that, at least in Adams's mind, the impediment had already disappeared. It just required some patience and a little more time to manifest. Whenever people asked if he had a speech impediment, he responded cheerfully with, "What? No!"

On summer vacations, Adams cut his entrepreneurial teeth working in his father's ice business. They distributed ice throughout the rest of Iowa—to gas stations, convenience stores, and anywhere else it was needed. "If you can sell ice, you can sell anything," his father used to say. Adams felt the lisp impeded him from being an effective salesperson, so he continued his practice behind closed doors: "*S, s, s, s,*" he would repeat, "*I am a great speaker. I am a great communicator. S, s, s, s...*"

Working with his father gave him exposure to all elements of an operating business, and together they grew Adams Ice Service to more than 100 accounts. Endeared to his father and happy to be of service, Adams would proudly draw pictures of himself in front of the ice truck, dreaming of one day owning the business himself so his father could retire.

Finally, just before starting college, his lisp faded and his confidence skyrocketed. Adams enjoyed college life—maybe too much, if the paltry 1.68 GPA in his freshman year was anything to go by. Fun took up the great majority of his time, leaving very little energy for study. While he persisted with college, he lacked purpose or ambition, simply accepting whatever grades came his way, until a chance encounter resurrected his entrepreneurial spirit.

One day, the 20-year-old attended a class presentation by eccentric entrepreneur and fellow Iowan "Cactus" Jack Barringer, regarded as an expert in product design and launch. Barringer assured Adams that a life beyond his wildest dreams lay ahead, if he had the discipline to make a few simple changes. The first step, he said, was to get a copy of *Think and Grow Rich*. "I read the book," Adams reflects, "and in that moment, I realized I was no different to Ford, Edison, and Carnegie: that I could achieve *anything* I set my mind to, regardless of my current situation." He also drew parallels between his own struggles with the speech impediment and the story of Hill's son, Blair, who transmuted significant physical ailment into advantage. Inspired and brimming with confidence, he replaced doubt and passiveness with faith and determination.

In the summer of 2011, with Barringer as his mentor, Adams came up with an idea for an innovative device that would cool and flavor bottled beverages—*ArcticStick* was born. To validate his idea, Adams entered an apprentice competition that would put the inventions and ideas of 250 people under the microscope of industry experts. Of those, only 50 would be selected to showcase their work in person, and only one would be crowned winner. Adams focused all of his efforts on a single goal with a set time constraint: *ArcticStick* was awarded first place in the competition, and Adams was given a $5,000 check to jumpstart his business and further develop the product. The victory increased his confidence even further and was tangible proof that indeed he could achieve anything to which he set his mind.

Assured that *ArcticStick* would be a popular product nationwide if enough people knew it existed, the young entrepreneur spent almost four years and more than $100,000 trying to make his project a success. Adams pitched it to everyone he met, eventually making it to *Shark Tank* casting calls and appearing on the cover of *USA Today*. "I convinced my mind I could do it, and I carried the product in my pocket like a crazy person," he says of this time. However, something unexpected happened: Adams noticed that people started to gravitate toward him rather than the actual product, giving him peace of mind that if *ArcticStick* failed, he could refocus his efforts and come up with something better.

With *ArcticStick* not yet to market, Barringer approached him with an idea of establishing their own product development company, offering Adams the opportunity to buy out the great majority of patents that Barringer himself had accumulated over the years. Without giving it much thought, Adams agreed. He quickly asked his girlfriend, Samantha, to move from Minnesota to Des Moines, Iowa, so they could be together while he launched the new venture. "There's a job in it for you!" he promised. He even had $750,000 raised to fund it. Three months in, with agreements lined up, leases signed, and everything ready, the 23-year-old felt an unusual hesitation. "If I want to do something, I want to go all in. This just didn't feel like something I could be passionate about long term," he thought.

Adams swallowed his pride and told Barringer he was reneging on the deal. He turned the business investment funds down and pondered how he would make the repayments on the apartment on which he had signed a 12-month lease. Worse yet, he'd disappointed his mentor, and the strain of the situation caused him and Samantha to eventually go their separate ways. "I hit rock bottom. I had nothing in my life," he confesses.

In 2014, he continued his solitary push with *ArcticStick*. Unable to obtain financing without giving up majority equity, he tried crowdfunding—a newly popular capital-raising strategy whereby anyone in the world can contribute financially to a new product or service without the entrepreneur having to give up any equity in the business. Adams's Kickstarter campaign raised $26,000 in 33 days from over 240 backers, surpassing his goal. With enough cash in the bank and a product that had been refined over three years, *ArcticStick* went to market.

On New Year's Eve of that same year, Adams reflected on his journey so far, as well as his strengths and passions. The grueling struggle of bringing his own product to market helped him realize that what he was most passionate about was helping other people achieve their dreams. He also knew that most crowdfunding campaigns failed because people simply lacked the guidance to properly execute them. That night, he set an ambitious goal to be the top crowdfunding expert in the world. With laser-like focus, he traveled the country with an insatiable appetite for learning, interviewing as many relevant people as he could find. His findings formed the basis of a formula that could help anyone obtain financing for a new project, which Adams published in his 2015 book, *Keys to the Crowd*.

Maintaining a frenetic work schedule, Adams began to establish a reputation as an entrepreneur to watch. He started his own podcast—*University of Young Entrepreneurs*, now *Live to Grind*—to help people get the resources they need to make their whole venture, not just the financing side, a success. Adams would get to know each guest he brought onto the podcast and look for ways they could work together, exponentially multiplying his reach. One such guest, John Lee Dumas from *Entrepreneur on Fire*, mentioned he was interested in releasing a book that outlined everything he'd learned from his own journey. Almost a year after Adams had set his New Year's Eve goal, Dumas and Adams launched the *Freedom Journal* on Kickstarter, which raised $100,000 in 33 hours and more than $450,000 within a month—one of the largest crowdfunding campaigns of its type in history. For Adams, his career path had been validated and it was time to set even loftier goals.

In 2016, Adams launched the *Young Entrepreneur Convention* in Iowa as an annual event to equip aspiring entrepreneurs with all the tools they need to make their business a success; with his speech impediment now a distant memory, Adams was on stage with his heroes sharing his extraordinary journey with more than 500 attendees. His unwavering self-belief, persistence, and specialized knowledge led to him raising more than $1.5 million in a single year, earning him the moniker "King of Crowdfunding."

Today, Brandon T. Adams is the founder of Accelerant Media Group, a consulting company with expertise in PR, video production, mainstream media, and crowdfunding to help other brands turbocharge their vision and grow exponentially. There are two prerequisites for people who wish to join his team—they must have read Napoleon Hill's *Think and Grow Rich* and Dale Carnegie's *How to Win Friends and Influence People*. The 27-year-old is also the executive producer and host of his own television show, *Ambitious Adventures*, which gives people unique insight into the daily grind of building a business, and frequently hosts webinars and podcasts to help the next generation of business leaders. In the next year, his burgeoning business empire is on track to cross eight figures in revenue. By his fortieth birthday, Adams hopes to have positively impacted the lives of more than one billion people.

He and "Cactus" Jack Barringer are back on good terms and enjoy helping each other with a wide variety of projects. Adams also reconnected with Samantha, crediting her influence and inspiration as one of the most important elements in his success; today, their love is stronger than ever, and in 2018 they plan to live in 12 cities across the United States while filming their own reality television show, *Success in the City*. Reflecting on the rock-bottom period in his life, Adams now views it as the best thing that ever happened to him. He also fulfilled his childhood dream of taking over the family ice distributorship and is excited to lead the second-generation business into the future.

With a grandiose vision and the right team in place, Adams is more motivated than ever. "After all," he says, "if you never stop, no one can beat you."

THE POWER OF THE MASTERMIND
THE DRIVING FORCE

"No individual has sufficient experience, education, native ability, and knowledge to ensure the accumulation of a great fortune, without the cooperation of other people."
—NAPOLEON HILL

GREAT SUCCESS NEVER COMES SOLELY ON THE BACK OF one's own efforts. The power of the mastermind is unleashed when efforts toward a common purpose are aligned, exponentially amplifying its reach.

Two elements, when brought together, create a third element. A practical illustration can be seen in one of the strongest horses in the world, the Belgian draft horse. One Belgian draft horse alone can pull 8,000 pounds. Two Belgian draft horses who are not familiar with each other can pull up to 24,000 pounds. Incredibly, two who are raised and trained together can pull 32,000 pounds— four times that of a single horse.

More and more studies have highlighted the importance of a diverse, highly motivated group for optimal results. When it comes to building your own team of influence, not all are created equal. Your mastermind must be comprised of those who are coordinated, in a spirit of harmony, toward a definite purpose. In the free market, those who ignore this principle will inevitably find themselves tied to the tracks as a thundering locomotive approaches. Instead, use the power of the mastermind to build your own locomotive.

A mastermind may take many forms: friends, a spouse, a business partner, a management team, an entrepreneurs network, a mentor, or even a protégé. Think back over the stories you have read: Jim Stovall's first mastermind partners were his protégé Christopher and his mentor Lee Braxton; Lewis Howes and John Lee Dumas tapped every guest they had on their podcasts as part of their mastermind group; and for Rob Dyrdek it was Jimmy George, the DC team, and George Pratt.

Power, in Hill's sense, is defined as "organized and intelligently directed knowledge." Elon Musk may have created Tesla, but he no sooner built each vehicle than he did the rocket that took his other company, SpaceX, into orbit. Musk achieved his goals by boldly declaring his definite purpose to the world, surrounding himself with people who could provide the knowledge he needed (and help organize it into clear plans), and then went to work on making his dream a reality. What is far less reported is how perilously close Musk came to ruin. But he persisted, learned from his failures, held unwavering faith, and as a result has completely revolutionized numerous industries, making himself an enormous fortune in the process. In fact, Musk's last decade may be the best modern-day example of the entire achievement philosophy.

Even the grandest, most intricate plans will flounder without sufficient means to translate them into action. However, those who harness the true power of the mastermind change the world.

Tim Storey

It was business as usual in Compton, California. At 7 A.M., palm trees stood tall and the sun glistened on car windshields as the city's notorious traffic started to build. Inside a two-bedroom house in a low-income neighborhood, the Storey family were in the middle of their own rush hour as they prepared for the school day.

A knock at the front door scarcely interrupted the household bustle. Only Bessie—the mother of the five young children inside—took any notice. It was uncharacteristically early for visitors.

"Ma'am, is your husband Anthony Storey?" the police officer asked.

Bessie nodded.

Her next duty would be to tell her children that their father was not coming home that day. Anthony Storey had been killed in a freak automobile accident.

In the coming months, the Storey family dealt with the news as best they could—as well as anyone could. The tragedy became the elephant in the room. While they felt the pain, they could not talk about it and certainly did not know how to work through it. The bubbly, outwardly jovial family had lost its spirit.

Anthony and Bessie had both left school early, holding tenth- and sixth-grade educations, respectively. Anthony's job as a steelworker had kept food on the table and, while far from wealthy, the family had always been happy. Bessie's meagre wage from working at a local donut shop just wasn't enough, and the unexpected death of her husband crippled her on many fronts. Suddenly, putting food on the table and being solely responsible for five young children seemed an insurmountable hurdle.

For 10-year-old Tim Storey, school was a welcome distraction. He focused on everything else in his life and tried to enjoy a normal upbringing: playing sports, listening to his favorite Motown music, and learning to dance.

Two years later, the first of a series of mentors appeared in Storey's life: one of his sixth-grade teachers took a liking to him. This man knew what had happened to Storey's father and had noticed that the boy was still struggling with grief. The teacher recommended he immerse himself in books—mainly biographies of people who had succeeded despite extreme adversity— and encouraged him to follow his passion. For the first time, someone outside his family believed in him enough that he felt any path was possible if he had the courage to pursue it. The stories of historical luminaries Winston Churchill, Abraham Lincoln, and George Washington inspired him to think bigger than his circumstances.

Storey felt his life turn a corner, but then his family faced another tragedy. Just two years after the accident that killed their father, one of Storey's sisters was killed in another automobile accident. Storey had matured and toughened in that time, and he now felt able to lead his family through the difficult period. He had developed coping mechanisms that allowed him to feel loss and appreciate grief for what it was. Somehow, he knew the family would get through it, and better than they had done before. Despite his youth, Storey was able to act as a rudder for his family—especially his mother—and the family coped.

A few years later, he walked into a local restaurant and observed that the tables were a mess. A lone busboy slunk through the restaurant, not showing much enthusiasm for the task at hand. Storey approached the restaurant owner, Mr. Anderson, and said, "Sir, my name is Timmy Storey. I want you to know that if I worked for you, your tables would never look like this." Anderson replied, "When can you start?"

For 15-year-old Storey, this was much more than just his first paid job. Anderson was a successful restauranteur who dressed well and spoke eloquently and would serve as another mentor for the impressionable teenager.

"He cared about me enough to try to bring the best out in me," Storey fondly remembers.

After an 18-month stint where he worked through the ranks—from dishwasher to busboy to waiter—Storey received a job offer from a different restaurant and went forth with Anderson's blessing: "Timmy, you've been one of my best employees ever. I want every success for you. Go ahead, you're stepping up."

In his final years of high school, Storey began to think about what he wanted for the rest of his life. One teacher he greatly respected had noticed Storey's spiritual side and desire to help people. He mentioned that Storey might enjoy humanitarian work and perhaps even seminary. With his high school diploma secured, Storey enrolled in Southeastern University in Lakeland, Florida, where he would obtain a Bachelor of Arts, majoring in religion.

After college, Storey succumbed to his burning desire to travel and began to explore the world. His first trip outside the United States was to Sweden, where, at 20 years of age, he spoke in public schools on motivation, success, and persisting with your dreams. Over the next year, in his first official humanitarian efforts—and in stark juxtaposition with affluent Sweden—he visited orphanages in Nigeria and prisons in the Philippines.

Meeting forgotten people in two of the world's poorest countries opened his eyes to a truth he had not previously encountered—that everyone in the world grows up with one of two primary motivators: "want" or "desire." As a child, Storey's want was guidance and to get out of the situation he was in. Now his desire was to give others the kind of guidance he had needed. For the poor communities he visited, though, their want was not just guidance, but water and food as well—a parallel but amplified version of his own beginnings. It gave Storey a sense of gratitude for his upbringing, which at one stage he had felt ashamed of.

Returning to the United States, Storey moved back to California and set up a headquarters for his growing life coaching business. His speaking tours took him around the country and eventually the world, where he motivated and inspired tens of thousands of people to think bigger than their circumstances.

In 1992, Dyan Cannon, ex-wife of Hollywood heart-throb Cary Grant, approached him: "Tim, I've seen you speak before and I really like where you're coming from—you're spiritual but not religious. I'm thinking of having a spiritual gathering at my house and would love you there."

Storey accepted the invitation, and it proved to be a pivotal moment. From his friendship with Cannon, he was introduced to some of the biggest film stars on the planet—Walter Matthau, Jack Lemmon, Elliot Gould, James Caan...Storey started a regular "Study" meeting, to which they flocked. In a city of glitz and glamor, they were drawn to Storey's life coaching skills and how he interpreted simple songs and proverbs for everyday use.

In 1994, at the age of 34, he wrote his first book, *Good Idea or God Idea?*, endorsed by business magnate Lee Iacocca, with whom Storey had worked intermittently. With this encouragement, Storey began to pursue bigger dreams, which led him to the home of Quincy

Jones, winner of 28 Grammy Awards and one of the most iconic figures in music. Jones began to refer to Storey as "The Voice" and became an important mentor for Storey when it seemed he had achieved all he could.

"It built my faith and expanded my thoughts of what I could accomplish," Storey says of Iacocca and Jones's contributions at that stage of his life.

Storey was now rubbing shoulders with some of the most accomplished people in the world, and every conversation honed his coaching skills. His regular "Study" meeting continued to attract the A-list crowd, and he taught them to find balance in their lives: physical, mental, spiritual, social, financial, and family.

One day Storey's phone rang. On the other end was a mutual friend who asked him to meet with Robert Downey Jr.—the infinitely talented but deeply troubled actor. It was 1999, and pre-superhero Downey Jr. had enjoyed onscreen success but just could not get his life into gear. His drug addiction led to him violating the terms of his probation, and he had been sent to a state prison in Corcoran, California. The despondent actor explained his actions to the judge: "It's like I've got a shotgun in my mouth with my finger on the trigger, and I like the taste of the gun metal." His wife had left him, and his career looked to be in tatters.

On his way to a meeting with the Oakland Raiders NFL team, Storey dropped in to the prison and met with Downey Jr. After listening to the embattled actor share his struggles, Storey counseled: "Stop looking back at your life, and don't let your setbacks define you. I know you're hurting right now, but the bigger the mess, the bigger the message. The bigger the test, the bigger the testimony. The bigger the setback, the bigger the *comeback*."

They also spoke about being rich, but not in the financial sense. "Being truly rich is having an abundance of love, mercy, grace, gratitude, humility, and benevolence," Storey said. "When we're rich in that sense—regardless of how difficult our environment might be or what struggles we face—we are happy, accountable for our actions, and free to chart our own success."

The uplifting message that he could rise above his circumstances struck an instant chord with Downey Jr., who has since solidified himself as one of the most bankable figures in show business.

Several years later, Storey's world would change again quite coincidentally. He had just finished speaking at an event when Dianne Hudson, Oprah Winfrey's executive producer, approached him, insisting that they meet. The inspirational life coach and the talk show host met and found that they shared many ideas on how to make the world a better place. Not long after, Storey appeared on the *Super Soul Sunday* TV show with Winfrey, which shot him into a whole new sphere of success, introducing him to hundreds of millions of people.

Winfrey was the latest in a long line of mentors who spurred Storey on to think bigger than his circumstances, regardless of what he had accomplished.

The journey continues for the inspirational life coach, who has now visited 75 countries, written 9 bestselling books, and established himself as a spiritual leader for executives, celebrities, and athletes alike. But he still makes time for his number one passion: helping people of all backgrounds understand that when they're feeling the sting of setback, life is preparing their comeback.

David Meltzer

One evening, seven-year-old David Meltzer heard a sound coming from the kitchen. He peered in to see his mother, Karen, leaning against the broken dishwasher, quietly sobbing.

"What's wrong, mom?" the boy asked.

"Nothing, David. Everything is okay," she affirmed.

The boy stared for a moment, and then brought her into his arms. As they hugged, he whispered, "One day I'll buy you a house and you'll never have to worry about anything ever again."

Just two years earlier, Meltzer had seen his parents' relationship deteriorate, with his father's philandering being the catalyst for their divorce. The young boy made a promise to his dad that in his absence he would take care of his mother and step up to be man of the house. Insulted, his father responded with his hand.

It was a difficult time for Karen, now a single mother of six children and relying on her wages as a substitute teacher. But while they were short of money, she tried to make sure they were never short of love and encouragement.

During the week, Karen would pack the family's dinners—usually peanut butter and jelly sandwiches— into brown paper bags and drive to her second job. While she worked inside at the convenience store and the rest of the family waited in the car, she encouraged the older kids to read to their younger siblings so they could connect as a family and expand their minds.

Too young to factor in the complexities of the world, Meltzer believed that financial wealth was the sole key to his mother's happiness. Seeing her secretly weep over another broken appliance they couldn't afford to fix broke his heart, and he made a vow to be a mega-success as soon as possible. He also wanted to do it ethically, to prove to his father that success and integrity weren't mutually exclusive.

At the age of 10, Meltzer stumbled across a poem called "Don't Quit," which impressed him so much he simply tore it out of the book.[6] It remained in his pocket everywhere he went, acting as a rudder to keep his aspirations on track. Each adversity caused him to refocus on the end goal, creating an ultra-competitive streak that complemented his energetic demeanor. "I wanted to be the best at everything," he recalls, "And I would not quit. I may not have been as intelligent or as athletic as the next guy, but one thing they couldn't do was outwork me."

His superior work ethic paid dividends through high school, and he decided that becoming a professional athlete was the quickest route to financial gain. Alas, in college, he came face to face with the brutish figures who would join him on the field. Physically, he was a long

---

6   A popular poem in the United States, of disputed authorship.

shot to make the team, let alone excel. Meltzer did make the team, but he realized that—for him at least—success lay elsewhere.

As college progressed, his focus turned to how he would make an impact in the business world. A friend gave him a copy of *Think and Grow Rich*, and it entered Meltzer's life at just the right time. He told the universe he would receive a job that would fulfill his ultimate goal to provide for his mother's future. Shortly after, two job offers fell into the lap of the third-year law student—one as an oil and gas litigator, and the other with a publishing company that was doubling down on the internet.

When he sought counsel from his mom, she responded convincingly. "The internet is a fad," she insisted. "Go with the oil and gas job for something solid."

He wanted to heed her advice, but instinct told him to get a second opinion. A conversation with his law school professor was equally firm. "Do not be an oil and gas litigator," Professor Yiannopolous urged. "You could sell ice to an Eskimo. Take the West Publishing role and use your sales skills. You'll enjoy it more." He accepted the role a short time later.

It was the early 1990s, the Web 1.0 era, where connection expansion and information application were the primary aims. The company he worked for, West Publishing, had embarked on an ambitious plan to post all their legal materials online, which could then be used by associations and corporations for legal research.

Meltzer was a salesperson, remunerated on the number of eyes he could get to the West Publishing database. The company had already established a reputation as the premier provider of legal materials—a near monopoly on the market.

"I carried an energy of belief that I was going to be successful, and in doing so I attracted what was going to manifest," he reasons. "I did that unconsciously at the time, but as I got older I understood it more and more." With an uncapped payment structure, he applied his unparalleled work ethic, creative flair, and unwavering self-belief to the role. The first month his paycheck was $33,000. Nine months later, he was a millionaire. It was another lesson for Meltzer, and one he'd encountered in Hill's book, about trusting his instinct over counsel. "Just because somebody loves you doesn't mean they have the situational knowledge to help you make the right decision," he realized.

When the company was sold in 1996, resulting in the retirement of much of the management team, Meltzer was left as the youngest executive in the company. He saw the incredible trajectory of the internet and, rather than return to law, decided to brand himself as an internet guru.

Despite not having any official experience or expertise in technology—at that point he was simply a high-performing salesperson—Meltzer applied for and was awarded a role as director of a wireless proxy server company, owned by consulting conglomerate Accenture. The internet continued to boom, and Meltzer used his presentation skills to raise more than $160 million to fund the company's innovation and expansion.

Next, he was headhunted by Samsung to roll out its first convergence device (now known as a smartphone) in the United States. The launch was a tremendous success and led to speaking gigs and other opportunities around the world. But it became clear that Meltzer still hadn't mastered the technical skills needed to grow the company into the new era. Management suspected the young CEO was out of his depth and brought in someone to replace him.

In 2003, Meltzer retired with a brimming bank balance. He could buy his family whatever they wanted, and did. He built his wife, Julie, her dream home, his mom the house he had promised her almost three decades earlier, and took his money out for a spin—buying luxury Italian sports cars, boats, and other toys.

The first night in his grandiose new residence, the 35-year-old tossed and turned. He looked to his wife and said, "I think I've made a big mistake."

"What do you mean?" Julie replied.

"I feel so empty," he said despondently.

To fill the void, and without any mentors to help him through this transition period, Meltzer started hanging out with a new group of super-wealthy, entitled friends.

They indulged in seedy nightclubs, recreational drugs, and excess liquor, and tried to outdo each other with materialism and ego. Each day of debauchery chipped away at the qualities that made Meltzer the man his wife and children adored—gratitude, empathy, accountability, and the ability to connect with people—attributes that had also made him a success in the business world. He was loose with his money, buying a ski mountain in Montana, 33 residential properties, and a golf course, which he then leveraged.

One morning, Meltzer came home and overhead a conversation between his wife and her uncle. She was visibly upset, and in between sobs he heard, "I'm really worried. I'm not sure if Dave can pull himself out of what's going on."

They realized Meltzer could hear their conversation so decided to tackle the problem head on. "Do you even know who you've become?" Julie pleaded, and outlined the actions that justified her concern.

"How can you say this to me!?" Meltzer responded angrily. "Look around you," he said, gesturing to the extravagant house and fleet of luxury cars. "How can you not be happy?"

"Are you kidding me?" Julie said.

Meltzer stormed out. A few hours later, he met his oldest and dearest friend for a round of golf. On the first tee, Meltzer asked, "Why don't you hang out with me anymore?"

"I just don't like who you hang out with."

"I'm not like those guys," Meltzer said.

"You can lie to me, but don't lie to yourself," his friend responded.

In one day, his wife and best friend had delivered a one-two combination to Meltzer's heart. It was time for change.

That afternoon, he apologized to his wife, who encouraged him to take stock of who he was and, more importantly, who he wanted to be. It was the only way they could keep their family together. Meltzer conducted a self-audit to find out what went wrong, cut ties with the negative influences with which he had recently surrounded himself, and sought to get his old self back.

As he focused intensely on becoming a better father and husband once more, his rampant expenditure came home to roost. He was declared bankrupt, and the bank repossessed everything they had.

Despite the challenging circumstances, Meltzer estimated that with the right plan, hard work, and a positive mental attitude, something would manifest soon. For the next six months, in far more modest surroundings, Meltzer stuck to his guns. When people asked how he was, he would say, "Terrific! Never better." He started meditating on what role he would play in the world. One day the phone rang. A leading mobile application company offered him a role as head of their game division, which involved expanding their presence internationally. He accepted, agreeing to start in two weeks' time.

The next day, a high school friend rang Meltzer from London and asked if he could fly out to negotiate on his behalf for a reality television show with Magic Johnson, being represented by sports superagent Leigh Steinberg—the inspiration for blockbuster film *Jerry Maguire*.

"You realize I'm not a real lawyer," Meltzer told his friend.

"You're the best negotiator I've ever seen. I want you representing me," his friend insisted.

Meltzer packed a bag and called a taxi. "Don't do anything stupid," his wife warned.

"I'm just going to help a friend!" Meltzer reassured.

In London, he met with Steinberg, and the pair instantly hit it off. Their first meeting lasted seven hours, and Steinberg phoned the next morning to ask if they could catch up again that day. After the meeting, Meltzer flew back to California and told his wife he was now the chief operating officer at the world's leading sports management agency.

As his tenure in the new industry started, Meltzer felt alive. He was mentally and spiritually in the best place he'd ever been in and was excited to make a difference. Within six months he was named CEO and negotiated more than $2 billion in sports and entertainment contracts.

However, for years rumors had circulated about Steinberg's drinking; it was the industry's worst kept secret. After one heavy bout, Meltzer and Warren Moon—Hall of Fame NFL player—decided they would leave for a healthier environment. In 2010, they set up their own company, Sports 1 Marketing, which would leverage their relationships with athletes and celebrities to help those most in need.

In seven years, Sports 1 Marketing has raised tens of millions of dollars for charity, awarded and funded hundreds of college scholarships, and given hundreds of people opportunity, experience, and employment via their robust internship program. More importantly, Meltzer and Moon have proven the model of compassionate capitalism—that offering service and value to other people first can lead to success for all stakeholders.

From a young age, establishing a true connection with a constant stream of mentors—including school teachers, university professors, and business leaders—helped Meltzer continually grow, jump outside his comfort zone, and have faith through the darkest times. Today, he believes each person needs three mentors at all times to help them achieve sustained wealth in all areas of their lives.

Daily practices of meditation, gratitude, and purpose have led to a stronger-than-ever connection with his family, including the once-strained relationship with his father. After having ridden the rollercoaster of failure and success, it's Meltzer's personal mission to help people enjoy the pursuit of their potential, which life has taught him is the surest path to happiness.

Just shy of his fiftieth birthday, David Meltzer is more peaceful and productive than ever before, knowing a big bank balance means nothing if the rest of your life is a mess.

—☙—

THE MYSTERY OF SEX TRANSMUTATION
CONVERTING ENERGY TO OUTPUT

—☙—

*"There is no other road to genius than
through voluntary self effort."*
—NAPOLEON HILL

AS INDIVIDUALS, NATURE HAS GIVEN US ALL WE NEED to succeed, just as we have all we need to implode—the universe simply responds to the dominating thoughts of our subconscious. Human sexual desire can be compared to water. Arguably the most persistent substance on earth, water will search for an outlet at all costs, even when blocked. When harnessed and directed, it can be an extremely formidable asset, capable of everything from helping maintain human physiological function to transporting essential nutrients to plants. With the right structure in place, water can even be converted for use as electricity.

Through willpower, our strongest desires can be channeled into constructive and effective action. Mastery of this principle ignites several valuable attributes within the human spirit, such as imagination, courage, and creative ability, and directs them toward a different endgame to something far more profound. When mastered by desires, however—without learning how to transmute them when appropriate—destruction can soon follow. Whether it is sex, drugs, or ego, those who never learn to harness their will and transmute their impulses may lose everything as they live from one "fix" to another, sabotaging their successes and leaving a trail of carnage in their wake.

As many of these stories demonstrate, desires can be exacerbated or diminished by one's surroundings, which is why choosing your friends and environment are so important. Technology also offers today's generations many easy outlets for impulses that, if not checked, can serve as an ongoing distraction to your definite purpose.

Interestingly, most only develop the willpower and properly understand this principle in their thirties, paving the way for their life's work to manifest in the decades following.

Sexual expression is part of our DNA, and for many, success comes on the back of inspiration drawn from a healthy relationship or the excitement surrounding a new relationship. Even the memory of love can be enough to parlay one's own circumstances into superior creative effort. In almost all cases, those who have risen to the highest of heights did so with the prolonged support and healthy influence of a life partner.

Of sexual expression, Hill wrote: "This desire, when harnessed and transmuted into action, other than that of physical expression, may raise one to the status of genius." It is the hallmark of personal magnetism— the basis of human interaction—and if properly wielded can turn charisma, confidence, enthusiasm, and presence into enormous financial reward or movements that start a revolution.

All it takes is the willpower to make it happen.

John Shin

John Shin heard the commotion and looked back. "Oh no, not again," he groaned. Headed in his direction were the motley crew of bullies who'd been terrorizing him for months. Being the only Asian kid at school had made him a popular target. Shin turned and pedaled his bike as fast as his little eight-year-old legs could go. When he could pedal no more, he fell off his bike and stood hunched over. His legs trembled and his lungs screamed for air.

"Let's see what you got!" one of the bullies shouted, pushing Shin to the ground. "You look like Bruce Lee. Can you fight like him, too?" another taunted.

The young boy had no reply—verbally or physically. He simply took every punch and kick launched in his direction.

After the beating, Shin rode home dejectedly and gave his mother a sanitized version of the story. But his body told her a truer story. "That's it. We're enrolling you in martial arts class, starting tomorrow," she said.

Eight years earlier, the Shins had left their life in South Korea and moved to Los Angeles in search of better opportunities for their two children, John and Stella. Both parents worked two jobs not only to put food on the table but also to save for their children's college fund. Each sacrifice felt justified because they believed fervently that their children would one day succeed in their own careers, as lawyers or doctors. But John's schooling being interrupted by bullies? That was unacceptable. Mrs. Shin grabbed the phone and booked John into a martial arts school.

Next afternoon, a van from the martial arts center collected students from local schools and dropped them to the *dojang* for training. Shin began to spend most of his time there, not leaving until 10:30 P.M., when his parents would pick him up on their way home from work. It was at the training hall that he did his homework and practiced the three martial arts on offer: taekwondo, hapkido, and judo. If his parents advised that Shin had acted out or needed punishment for something, they left it to the master to determine the appropriate level and method of discipline.

The training hall quickly became Shin's second home, and he enjoyed making new friends there. Despite occasionally being on the receiving end of strict discipline, Shin developed great admiration for his master, who would teach the students three core lessons every single day: patience, respect, and humility. As his skills grew, he entered some local competitions, which built his confidence.

At 11, he won state and regional competitions, and three years later he took gold at the national competition. Shin then went on to compete at the World

Games and Pan American Games, with podium finishes in each.

In 1988, Shin was invited to try out for the judo team that would compete at the Olympic Games later that year in his birth nation, South Korea. In the months leading up to the selection, however, he started to mix with people who were more interested in having a good time than delivering a top performance.

To fit in with his new friends, Shin began smoking and quickly found himself getting through a pack of cigarettes a day.

Despite his new habit, he made it through to the quarter finals, where he encountered an opponent he'd handily accounted for at the earlier Pan American Games. But he felt different. Like his young self pedaling hard to evade the bullies, his lungs were screaming. And he knew that none of his competitors would pick up a habit as bad as smoking, given how focused they were on their athletic aspirations. "I got very complacent and felt invisible, and it ruined my entire judo career," Shin laments. With his dreams up in smoke, it was back to the drawing board.

While his parents still urged him to pursue a career in law, Shin instead applied for jobs with the CIA and FBI, believing his martial arts background might be a valuable skill. But without a master's degree or doctorate, they would not grant him so much as an interview. When he asked what course would boost his employment prospects in that field, the response was direct: "Law," they replied. Finally, after 21 years of coaxing from his parents, Shin enrolled in law school.

The program was a means to an end for Shin, and he grew frustrated learning about the ins and outs of contractual and constitutional law—but he persisted. After graduation, he obtained a job in Orange County as deputy to the district attorney. The day-to-day life of a lawyer seemed as drab and frustrating as law school. He worked hard and it made his parents happy, but he came home miserable. "What's the point of all this if, at the end of the day, I'm not happy?" he pondered.

In February 1994, he met Arlene, who also came from a legal background but had pursued a career in the financial services industry. After six months of dating, John and Arlene married. Together, they mapped out a life plan for their next five years, ten years, and beyond. Shin persisted in law but still hated it. One day it occurred to them that Arlene's salary surpassed John's. She suggested he attend a financial services conference to learn more about the industry and consider a career change. At that point, he dreaded the idea of even setting foot in a law office again, so the husband-and-wife duo started their own financial services business.

The first five years were a constant struggle to get their new venture off the ground. Arlene ran the office, while Shin spent most of the year in airplanes, trains, and cars, prospecting around the country. When he returned to their office in Cerritos, in suburban Los Angeles, he and Arlene worked so tirelessly they would often sleep on site.

Slowly, they began to build a client base, but the constant travel started to wear Shin down. One day he was sitting in a rental car outside a shopping center, wearing a suit and eating Burger King. "Is this really worth it?" he thought, the same negative affirmation that had entered his head every day for five years, urging him to quit. "If I do what everyone else does, I can go home at 5 P.M."

It was like a tennis match in his head, between positive and negative self-talk. "I refuse to be like everyone else. This *will* pay off!" his positive self countered. Once more he shook off the negative chatter, clinging to his faith that putting everything he had into each day would yield exponential results in due course.

Business started to grow, but the Shins were putting in way too much time for the results they were getting—especially with the demands of a young family. It was the most difficult time in their lives, but they supported each other to remain laser-focused on their goals. Later that year they qualified for a trip to Hawaii with the licensee with which their business was affiliated. Sitting poolside on the first day, they flipped open the menu and saw the price of a cheeseburger was $20. "How are we going to see out the week if the food is this expensive?" Shin asked his wife.

That afternoon, they saw one of the founders of the company, Monte Holm, walk by and decided to share their concerns. "We're working so hard, but we're barely making headway. Can you give us any advice?" they pleaded.

"Enjoy Hawaii and sharpen your axe," Holm replied. The couple stared back at him, stumped.

"If we work too hard, we can continue chopping the tree, but eventually our axe becomes dull," he explained. "At that point, you're not cutting the tree down. The tree is cutting you down. Sharpen your axe in Hawaii, and I'll be in touch when you get back to California."

So, the Shins did their best to relax and enjoy their vacation. When they returned to Los Angeles they received the promised call: "Mr. Shin, Monte Holm would like you to come out to his house in Utah."

Shin paused. Their time in Hawaii had eroded their savings, especially since they weren't earning any income during the time they were away. "I would love to, and really appreciate the gesture. But unfortunately I don't have the money to get there," Shin said.

"Don't worry," came the reply, "Monte will send his plane out."

Holm's private jet picked Shin up at Van Nuys Airport and flew him to Utah to meet the man who seemed to have the whole world figured out. He spent three days at Holm's place, discussing what strategies were needed to make not only his business, but his life, a success.

At the end of the trip, before getting back on the plane, Holm had one more piece of advice. "You also need to read *Think and Grow Rich*," he said. Shin nodded and boarded the plane. It was a sentence that would transform his life.

Thinking about what resources he had at his disposal, Shin read the recommended book carefully. These words leapt out at him:

> *The "Master Mind" is the coordination of knowledge and effort, in a spirit of harmony, between two or more people, for the attainment of a definite purpose. This form of cooperative alliance has been the basis of nearly every great fortune, and the source to which the genius turns.*

Shin committed to surrounding himself with those seeking grander fortunes and willing to put in the work to achieve it. He told the financial advisers at their company that he was creating a 90-day boot camp that would meet each fortnight from 3 P.M. to midnight, conceptually congruent to the elite branches of the military. The ones who stuck it through would be part of his "Inner Circle" and receive ongoing access to unparalleled growth opportunities.

Sure enough, the group shrank a little after each meeting, as many complained about the work, the hours, and the disruption. Finally, Shin was left with a core group of go-getters who shared a common trait—a tenacious appetite for success—yet differed in just about every other way, including age, gender, religion, ethnicity, and educational background. "It doesn't matter who you are," Shin told his group. "Success does not discriminate. It will come to all those who do what needs to be done."

They continued to meet and help each other achieve individual success. Three months later, they topped the rankings as the best-performing advisers in his company. Shin ran the Inner Circle program again and again—sure enough, each time he got the same result. After the fifth time, Shin's phone rang—the licensee asked if he could teach his methods nationwide.

John and Arlene Shin's unbreakable bond continues to this day. Their business has been operating for 23 years, has grown to more than 1,000 locations, and commands a 7,000-strong legion of advisers throughout the United States and Canada. There's only one prerequisite for all new candidates who apply for a job there—they must have read *Think and Grow Rich*. Shin has also mentored thousands of people to help them become successful business owners.

Avid philanthropists, the Shins have constructed numerous orphanages in some of the poorest countries on earth and helped thousands of children develop a sense of hope and self-worth. Shin has not forgotten the bullying he endured in elementary school, and he's on a quest to show people that—regardless of background or circumstance—with a little help and the right plan, the possibilities are endless.

Lionel Sosa

"If you want to be successful," Roberto told his 12-year-old son, "create something, go where the money is, and get along with as many people as possible." Lionel Sosa nodded. It was his first day working in the family laundromat and a lesson that he would remember for the rest of his life.

Roberto had just moved his family to an affluent suburb of San Antonio, Texas, to open the business, a laundromat he named Prospect Hill Cleaners to avoid any stigma associated with his own, far more Latino-sounding name. He recognized that higher-income neighborhoods offered the best opportunity to make the laundromat a success, as they would have more articles to clean and the disposable income to outsource it locally. At the time, the Sosas were the only Mexican family to own a business in Prospect Hill and the only Mexican family to live there. Sosa began working in the business as a teenager, helping his father with anything that needed doing. The real-world apprenticeship showed him the value of getting along with as many people as possible, regardless of ethnicity, gender, vocation, or net worth. It meant a larger base of prospective clients, which translated to a larger share of an ever-growing demand.

As the son of immigrants, Sosa had an upbringing that mixed his family's Mexican roots with the distinctive culture of San Antonio. While his father continually advised him to follow his artistic talent and be friends with everyone to increase his chances of opportunity, it was his mother who drilled into him the work ethic required if he wanted to be successful. "As a Latino, you need to work harder, much harder, if you want the same opportunities. Always be at least twice as good," she would say. "Make it hard for them to ignore you."

Sosa loved watching his father draw intricate sketches and soon found that he too had artistic talent. He attended a vocational high school, one where—outside of a basic core curriculum—much of the emphasis was placed on trades and blue-collar work, such as carpentry, automobile mechanics, and upholstery. For Sosa, subject choices were easy. Year after year he opted for the commercial arts program, spending three hours a day refining his creative flair. Roberto would paint over the brick wall in the back of the family laundromat with a light color, playfully challenging his son to convert the blank canvas into something special.

After high school, Sosa obtained a job at Texas Neon Sign Company, where he was paid $1.10 an hour to design signs that were then manufactured and erected on shopfronts and buildings throughout San Antonio. Sosa also married Kathy, the love of his life, and they started a family of their own. Throughout his time at the sign shop, he developed a close bond with 39-year-old colleague Leonard Dyke, who was born to a wealthy family and had a very strong network throughout the city.

One day, Leonard said, "Lionel, you're a pretty smart guy. Why are you working for these miserable wages?"

Sosa said, "This is not miserable. This is a fun job!"

"You don't get it," Dyke replied. "You could be earning a lot more. From now on, every Wednesday, I'm going to take you to lunch with friends of mine who are making so much money it will make your head spin."

As promised, Dyke took his friend out to lunch and introduced him to as many people as he could. Each week, Dyke told Sosa that the people they met for lunch were no smarter than him but were making six, seven, eight times as much in each paycheck. "They're not geniuses. They're just regular people," he told the young signwriter.

Just a few weeks later, Sosa heard a woman speaking with the sales staff in the adjoining office. Their conversation flowed through the open door, and he overhead her say, "I want to order a small sign for my new business downtown—the Napoleon Hill School of Personal Achievement." After the meeting, Sosa walked out and introduced himself.

"Could you please tell me what this school is about?" he asked.

"Simple. We teach people to be millionaires," she replied. It seemed such an odd coincidence, having this woman come into the office so soon after Dyke had opened his eyes to what could be possible with a little help, that Sosa decided to enroll and came up with a plan to gather the tuition fees.

The 26-year-old went to the bank with his father, who verbally guaranteed Sosa was no risk for the bank. "I will not co-sign this for him because he needs to learn on his own, but like me he's a man of his word— he'll pay back every penny." It was 1966, a different era in banking, and a handshake secured the deal. With the bank's $250, Sosa enrolled in the 17-week program. From the moment he learned the success principles, he began to apply them to all areas of his life. He founded Sosa Art (later SosArt) with the definite purpose of being the biggest and best graphics studio in Texas within five years, hoping to pay himself $2.50 an hour, double the minimum wage at the time. As he got more comfortable and more successful, his income aspirations broadened.

As the years ticked by and his business grew, Sosa continued to work hard. He was determined to surround himself with people who could turbocharge his skills, so he partnered with a friend from high school, Lupe Garcia, who led the charge on the graphics side, while Sosa drummed up business using what he had learned during the 17-week program. The business grew to 25 staff, and one day he looked at the calendar. "By golly, in five years, it happened," Sosa recalls with a grin. He was at the helm of the largest graphics studio in the state.

Three years after achieving his goal, Sosa felt advertising was a booming industry that would provide much more opportunity. Graphics work had been good to him, but it was just one component. Broadening their scope to focus on advertising would mean they could add value across the marketing spectrum, offering expertise in both radio and television commercials. To solidify the pivot, Sosa and Garcia merged their business with an existing agency led by Beverly Coiner and Warren Stewart, who had worked with some of the best creative talents in the world: Ed Yardang & Associates was born. They collaborated on a unified vision: to become the biggest and best advertising agency in San Antonio within five years. While it took them eight years to achieve their goal, they established a reputation as one of the state's premier ad agencies and, with their staff of 75, swept all the major creative awards.

In the late 1970s, Sosa started to hear about the growth of the Latino market and the significance it would play in the advertising industry. In 1978, the company received a phone call from a reputable US politician, John Tower, who was seeking their help with his upcoming election. Tower had been elected the first Republican United States senator from Texas since Reconstruction. At the time, all the South—from Florida to Texas—was regarded as solid Democratic states. The enigmatic senator had a bilingual education, fought for integration, and welcomed Latinos to Texas, successfully predicting their rise as the new middle class statewide. But despite winning the two previous elections, Tower's camp felt momentum had shifted to his opponent. They believed that shoring up a strong percentage of the Latino vote could make all the difference, although no prominent Republican candidate had targeted that segment before. Sosa and his colleagues were encouraged to make a pitch and won the business despite having no political experience between them.

As the campaign started, Tower's team became so convinced of the abilities of Sosa's advertising team that instead of the original brief of producing materials only for the Latino market, they were tasked with producing all his election advertising. They started campaigning far earlier than any other candidate had done previously and recorded a catchy 60-second jingle that dominated airwaves—it was so prevalent that many thought it was an actual song rather than a paid endorsement for a US senator. The television commercials showed Tower actively involved in Latino communities and speaking to key associations. Eventually, their marketing mix was so successful that name recognition for the Republican candidate reached an all-time high. As the election results poured in, Tower was victorious, winning 37% of the Hispanic vote. No Republican in Texas had ever won more than 8% before.

The grateful US senator asked how he could ever repay them. "Well, you could help us get more business," Sosa responded. "I'll do you one better," Tower replied. "I'm going to give you publicity like you've never had before. I'm going to get your story in *The Wall Street Journal.*"

In the following months, the article was published, and word spread like wildfire about the Texas advertising agency that could sway elections. "They thought if we could persuade Latinos to vote Republican instead of Democrat, surely we could convince them to pick one consumer product over another," Sosa recalls. Soon, some of the world's most prominent brands—including Coca-Cola, Coors, and Bacardi—came calling for their advice on how to woo the Latino market. And they brought big budgets, too. The agency was typically remunerated via a 15% portion of each client's campaign expenditure, which hovered between $50,000 and $100,000. However, after their successful partnership with Tower, these bigger companies brought in budgets of $5 million to $8 million per year. Their company suddenly had more business from three clients than it had had from all its previous clients combined.

Sosa's business partners weren't keen to focus solely on the Latino market, so the budding advertising guru sold his shares in the business and went out solo, launching Sosa & Associates in 1980 to help brands strike a chord with the Hispanic population. He was pulled back into the political realm when Tower referred him in glowing terms to another up-and-coming candidate, Ronald Reagan. The California Governor charged Sosa with leading Hispanic outreach for his successful initial

White House campaign in 1980. But it was his re-election bid in 1984 in which Sosa was given free reign, and a corresponding budget, to run his segment of the campaign the way he wanted. Sosa could see that nationwide, from California to Florida, the upwardly mobile Latino market was becoming more business-oriented and consuming more English-language media. Sosa ran his unique style of advertising, focusing primarily on battleground states with large Latino populations. The results came in, and it was a landslide victory for Reagan and the Republican Party.

To keep focus through all the turbulence of leaving one business, starting another, and skippering an entire segment for consecutive presidential elections, Sosa kept applying the blueprint inspired by Hill's program: make a goal, work ferociously, and never give up, no matter how hard it gets.

With two successful presidential campaigns under his belt, then President Reagan—who, after two terms, was ineligible for re-election—introduced Sosa to his vice president, George H. W. Bush. Sosa worked as the Hispanic outreach director for both of Bush's election bids and was successful in the first, but a spirited challenge from youthful Democratic candidate Bill Clinton brought the 12-year Republican run to an end. Sosa's own agency continued its rise to prominence, becoming the largest Hispanic ad agency in the United States, billing more than $100 million annually.

Sosa was recruited to assist George W. Bush in his last race for Texas governor, where Sosa's proven formula led to an even bigger share of the vote, amassing 49% of the Latino vote for the Republican incumbent. Sosa was then asked to join his team for the successful 2000 presidential race, and repeated their victory again four years later. Lionel Sosa, the son of immigrant parents and former signwriter from San Antonio, had risen above his modest upbringing to work on six presidential campaigns, winning five of them. He had also revolutionized an entire segment of the advertising industry.

In 2006, Sosa published *Think and Grow Rich: A Latino Choice*, a detailed insight into how he used Napoleon Hill's success principles to go from earning $1.10 an hour to living a prosperous life that influenced all echelons of society. To this day, he is most passionate about encouraging the Latino community to understand how consistent application of proven principles, embracing change, and collaborating with an effective team of high performers can transform the lives of all those who have the courage to think bigger than their circumstances.

Looking back on a remarkable life, Sosa regards his greatest accomplishment as the 30-year marriage he's shared with wife Kathy, from whom he's received a lifetime of unconditional love and support. Today, the couple share 8 children, 25 grandchildren, and 25 great-grandchildren.

THE SUBCONSCIOUS MIND
THE CONNECTING LINK

"The subconscious mind, alone, is the medium through which prayer may be transmitted to the source capable of answering prayer."
—NAPOLEON HILL

THE RELATIONSHIP BETWEEN DESIRE AND THE SUB-conscious mind can transcend illiteracy, poverty, and just about anything else. Consistently articulate what you want most, with perfect clarity, to allow the subconscious mind to absorb it on multiple fronts and turn it into ongoing, purposeful action.

As you study the achievement philosophy, you will start to recognize failure patterns in society. One of the most common examples can be seen in New Year's resolutions, especially those revolving around health and fitness. People making these goals often feel an emotionally charged intent, but unless the goal becomes an obsession and is reinforced with faith, organized planning, consistent action, and persistence, its probability of success is incredibly low—that is why gyms are empty in December and full in January. Another is the experience of those who expect earth-shifting results from prayer alone, often in response to fear and usually at the last minute. However, if properly used, the subconscious mind can translate almost any prayer into a definite plan to procure the object of the prayer.

Every great endeavor, innovation, or achievement once had its roots in a simple thought impulse. In your own quest, start small to build faith, but do not restrict your desires to things that are easily attainable. In Super Bowl LI, it was subconscious mastery that allowed New England Patriots' quarterback Tom Brady to stay calm and bide his time while the Atlanta Falcons ran riot. Trailing by 25 points in the third quarter, the 39-year-old had a single phrase looping through his head: "We just gotta score." Then he went to work, creating the opportunities that led the Patriots to victory—the largest comeback in Super Bowl history.

A well-conditioned subconscious will not prevent bad things from happening. Rather, it consistently redirects the energy associated with the event to more positive and productive means. In doing so, the probability of an enduring victory is greatly increased.

Errol Abramson

The Ferrari purred along the coastal road, drawing all eyes to its sleek contours and away from the waves rolling onto the shore. It was a sparkling summer day in Newport Beach, California; just the day for a drive.

Fourteen-year-old valet Errol Abramson watched the red speck turn into a brand-new 1964 *rosso corsa* Ferrari—his dream car. As it slowed and turned into the parking lot, Abramson counted his blessings. The vehicle pulled up to the restaurant and he excitedly opened the door, bidding the owner a good lunch. The young valet drove the Ferrari around the busy car park trying to find the perfect spot, pondering what glorious gratuity would await. "Ten dollars, twenty dollars...maybe even fifty!" he estimated.

He pulled up to a prime position, right in front of the restaurant, and returned to his post. As other vehicles arrived, Abramson waved his colleagues over, missing his turns. If he ignored any newcomers and remained within five feet of the keys at all times, he was bound to be the one called on to retrieve the sports car and collect the tip.

The Ferrari's owner finished his lunch and strolled toward the exit. Abramson scurried off, quickly returning with the car. He opened the door and eagerly awaited compensation.

The driver looked down, spotted a hole in Abramson's trousers, and pulled out a huge wad of cash. "He's going to buy me a new pair of pants," the boy thought. The man peeled off a crisp one-dollar bill and offered it to the young valet. Abramson's heart sank. He knew he should be grateful, but the disappointment was written all over his face.

Picking up on his attitude, the driver ripped the dollar out of the valet's hand. Abramson didn't know how to respond. After all, once the money was clenched in his palm, hadn't the exchange taken place and ownership been transferred? But now this wealthy man wanted to take the money away from someone who clearly needed it more.

The driver pulled out a gold pen, wrote something on the dollar bill, and handed it back, saying, "Son, you need an attitude adjustment. Read that book."

As the Ferrari sped out of his life, Abramson peered down at the money clasped in his hand. On it was written: *Think and Grow Rich. N. Hill.*

The next Saturday, Abramson found himself in front of a book store. He pulled out the dollar bill, which remarkably he hadn't yet spent, and walked into the store. He asked the cashier if they had *Think and Grow Rich* by N. Hill. They did, priced at 99 cents. Abramson slapped down the dollar and left the store, unsure what alchemy, if any, would transpire.

The 14-year-old was no stranger to adversity. He had a difficult upbringing, losing his mother at an early age and having a strained relationship with his father, who remained in Winnipeg, Canada. He lived alone in a shoddy apartment and worked as a valet and busboy to make ends meet. Abramson was also dyslexic, so reading of any kind made him uncomfortable. But he was curious to find out what the Ferrari driver knew that he didn't, so he opened the book. One slow page at a time, he read. As the weekend passed, he only left his apartment once—to buy a writing pad to take notes.

He skipped school on Monday to keep reading and finished the book the next day. The author promised that readers who captured the secrets sprinkled throughout the pages would unlock a surefire way to get anything they ever wanted. For a poor boy just one rung above street kid, it was captivating. He wrote down his wildest desires, no matter that many of them—like owning his own Ferrari—seemed fantastical given his current position.[7] Then he wrote down that he wanted to be a millionaire. Being wealthy, he thought, would give him the status and respect he craved.

On Wednesday morning he left his apartment and walked to school. On the way, he chuckled. Nothing had changed outwardly in his life, but for the first time ever he knew that he wasn't poor anymore. The book had

---

7 Abramson still scribbles ideas, no matter how far-fetched they seem, on notepads scattered throughout his house.

expanded the teenager's consciousness, and he was suddenly starting to see opportunities that he hoped would transmute into physical reward.

Two years later, Abramson had done as many odd jobs as he could to save up enough money for a grander opportunity. The real estate market was experiencing a seasonal boom, and he approached homeowners in northern Los Angeles who were looking to sell and began purchasing options (essentially the rights to the sale) on residential properties. He would offer the homeowner $1,000 for the option. If in 90 days he hadn't sold the option, the property owner would keep the $1,000. If the option did sell, the property owner wouldn't pay any real estate commission on the sale. Abramson's proceeds would be the difference between the forecast sale price of the property and the realized sale price of the property. It proved to be a winning formula, and he repeated it—44 times in a row—making a minimum of $5,000 per sale, far beyond his earning capability at the restaurant.

These victories had whet his appetite for larger deals. He used his financial windfall as a down payment on a derelict apartment complex, with the agreement for sale funded by rental incomes from the existing tenants. Five years after writing down his first ever financial goal, Errol Abramson was a millionaire.

While the 19-year-old had accumulated a large asset base and made significant inroads into living the life he wanted, he had little cashflow at his disposal. To alleviate this problem, Abramson started a vitamin business, using what was left of his free capital to purchase inventory and cover other setup costs. The majority of transactions were placed via mail order, meaning customers pre-paid for their products, providing a robust cash business for the budding entrepreneur.

He mirrored the success habits of every business leader he could find and asked what he could learn from their failures so he could avoid making the same mistakes. Reading still bothered him, but he attended as many quality seminars as he could to absorb the information in the most beneficial way.

The vitamin business expanded rapidly, and soon Abramson's stores were dotted around the city. He established some influential connections at a well-known radio station and held guest appearances at his own stores to boost sales. The company also started selling both wholesale and retail to maximize profits.

Rounding out the holistic strategy, Abramson founded a health magazine that increased consumer awareness around the supplement category. It attracted reputable medical practitioners to act as brand advocates for his vitamin products and offer content to legitimize the magazine. As the money poured in, he converted the apartment complex into condominiums and sold them for a tidy profit.

His business empire continued to expand, but he never took his foot off the personal improvement pedal.

If he didn't know how to do something, he would hire an expert in the field to either teach him how to do it or simply do it for him. Abramson's unrelenting action led to him making many mistakes, but he took it in his stride and viewed them as learning experiences—opportunities to revise his plans and advance.

Today, the eclectic entrepreneur has founded, purchased, and sold almost 50 companies across every major industry, including retail, real estate, finance, manufacturing, sports, health, and marketing. Four of the companies he founded have achieved more than $1 billion in annual sales.

For all his success, Abramson is most comfortable out of the limelight. After a period consulting to Fortune 500 companies, he now spends his time offering expertise to the small business sector and mentoring a growing team of aspiring business leaders. At the time of writing, he is also working on three startup companies.

Errol Abramson continues his mission to spread the *Think and Grow Rich* principles, having personally given away more than 1,000 copies of the book that transformed his life.

Blaine Bartlett

Blaine Bartlett pressed his face against the window, gazing down at the cities and towns that dotted the countryside as the airplane soared back to the United States. Nine months in Europe—his first overseas trip—had opened the 21-year-old's eyes to experiences, cultures, and opportunities he never knew existed. He grinned: the only thing he wanted for the rest of his life was to feel this alive.

Returning to Seattle, Washington, Bartlett accepted a job with the local newspaper to rebuild his bank balance and develop his business experience. During his first week, a colleague strolled through the office asking the employees if they'd like to contribute to a retirement gift for Reuben, one of their oldest staff members.

"How long has he worked here?" Bartlett asked.

"Fifty years," came the reply.

Bartlett feigned a smile, but it rattled him. It was common in that era to spend a long time in a secure job—many people had spent 10, 20, or 30 years with the family-owned newspaper, but 50 years was a *lifetime*.

Bartlett approached Reuben, who sat at a desk in a corner facing the wall, to get a sense of how he felt about his tenure and pending retirement. Reuben opined that his life was patterned, predictable, safe— just the way he liked it. Despite the assurances, and that Reuben was a likable chap, Bartlett's European adventure had changed his perspective. He saw something different: a rut. "That can't be me in 50 years," he thought. "It just can't."

Later that year, a friend invited Bartlett to a personal development training program in nearby Portland, Oregon. It was the early 1970s, and self-help was on its way to becoming a booming industry. The content struck an immediate chord with Bartlett: the notion that success does not discriminate by ethnicity, gender, or education; that we all have potential deep inside us waiting to be unlocked; and that success is available to all those who understand the formula for translating their potential to prosperity. These concepts suddenly crystallized everything Bartlett instinctively felt about success. The program ran for five days, and he excitedly signed up for the advanced course.

The second program was just as enlightening. The realization that he was the creator of his life—that with the right thinking he could literally have anything he ever wanted—affected the way Bartlett saw both space and time. For the next week he worked hard on a single focus: being truly present in the moment. "For that week, I felt awake for the first time in my life," he reflects.

His interest and passion for the workshop material led to Bartlett being offered a job with the company that facilitated the programs. The thought of speaking in front of more than two people at a time terrified the

22-year-old, but he was given training to overcome his fears. In particular, the encouragement and guidance of one woman in the company, Cara Foster, helped Bartlett get out of his comfort zone and build his confidence. It was Foster's mentoring that refined his presentation and engagement skills, which allowed him to travel the United States for the next five years, teaching the programs that had been so instrumental in changing his own life. Bartlett was also given more responsibility, eventually accepting more senior roles within the company's management.

As his growth plateaued, Bartlett felt the urge to move on the next challenge. He left the self-help industry and moved into financial services, selling mortgage-backed securities. It was an entirely different insight into the human psyche and showed him how people view money as a scarce resource, rather than something that can be attracted with the right thinking and planning.

In 1981, he received an invitation from his friend Dennis Becker to assist with a consulting project on the East Coast. He accepted the intriguing proposition, curious to see how applying his expertise in personal development might aid the corporate world. Their mission was simple to define but would be difficult to execute: they were to shut down, as cost-effectively as possible, a giant steel manufacturing mill in Buffalo, New York. Management and labor had been at loggerheads, and coupled with various macroeconomic factors the business had become untenable—the company had lost over a billion dollars in the previous year alone. Bartlett and Becker quickly recognized the disconnect between management and the heavily unionized labor force and created a program designed to increase both parties' awareness in a way that would enable them to make better choices now and in the future.

As they implemented the new program and relationships between management and labor began to improve, Bartlett and Becker realized they might be able to actually save some of the mill operations. After a year, drawing heavily on the principles Bartlett had been teaching to individuals, they were able to keep three mills in operation, save the company hundreds of millions of dollars, and keep thousands of jobs in the process. The success of that project showed Bartlett that if positive change could be effected in corporations, it would have ramifications for people all over the world.

After the East Coast assignment, Becker traveled to Japan to teach programs for individuals and suggested that Bartlett join him. Seeing the dramatic impact their teaching was having on individuals in an entirely different culture—communicating with Japanese audiences via an interpreter—was the final piece of evidence they needed. They prepared specialized programs tailor-made for the corporate world and offered their expertise to a whole new audience. Demand grew quicker than they could manage, and they kept up a rigorous teaching schedule throughout Japan and Hong Kong. Just three years later, they found themselves at the helm of the largest human resource consultancy program in Asia.

At 38 years old, Bartlett returned to the United States and set up his own company, Avatar Resources. He quickly attracted interest from major telecommunication companies and developed programs to help adjust their paradigms—how they thought about what they wanted—and align personal responsibility, choice, and awareness at each layer of the company. This multipronged approach unified the voices and interests of management and the workers, creating a symbiotic culture that would also be reflected in their balance sheets in the following years. Most importantly, people felt happier and more fulfilled in the workplace. Avatar Resources continued to grow, servicing clients throughout the United States, Japan, and Australia.

Through his work with these companies, Bartlett noticed that the mission of the business was often poorly translated into day-to-day actions—the two had become disconnected. "Is your organization a mission with a business or a business with a mission?" he would ask. That question helped reframe the thinking in companies where toxicity reigned and employees were regarded as disposable resources, to seeing them as a powerful asset that could be nurtured. Bartlett enjoyed the challenge of changing the very fabric of the business landscape—creating a winning culture and high profits concurrently—and continued to help as many people as he could.

In 2006, his personal fortitude was put to the test. His wife of 15 years, Pam, had been enduring increasingly debilitating back pain when Bartlett took her for treatment. The doctor was able to rule out some common afflictions but ordered a precautionary blood test, promising to be in touch when the results came in. The following day, Bartlett was at the pharmacy picking up muscle relaxants when his phone rang. "Stop what you're doing. We need you back here right away," the doctor instructed.

The couple braced for what was clearly going to be confronting news. "You have a form of cancer called multiple myeloma," the doctor said, before booking them in with an oncologist that afternoon. Despite major bouts of chemotherapy, a stem cell transplant, and more, nothing seemed to fight off the disease. Despite their comprehensive health insurance, restrictions existed for medical expenditure. As medication costs alone surpassed $15,000 each month, the couple found themselves in the fight for their lives, on multiple fronts.

Bartlett all but shut down his business while he focused on his wife's health and being the primary caregiver. Suddenly, helping companies reach their quarterly milestones seemed trivial compared to the very real struggle in his personal life. Despite Pam's valiant efforts, she passed away five years later. In that same period,

Bartlett's mother and father also passed. To cope with losing the woman who had been his rock for two decades, and his parents, who had given him their unconditional support throughout his life, he changed his daily routine. He began deep meditation and started to feel a spiritual connection between everything that happened in his life, regardless of how difficult, unfair, or cruel it seemed at the time.

This difficult period solidified Bartlett's belief that any capitalist society needed an inherently compassionate element. He says, "In today's world, business has the opportunity to fundamentally shift how we live on this planet. Compassion is needed now more than ever. Let's access the spirit of everything we do." He recalibrated his mission, gave greater weight to the compassionate element, and set out to help companies identify the spirit in everything they do—how to feel alive.

Today, through his work with business leaders, universities, and conferences, Bartlett has directly impacted the lives of millions. Aside from being regarded as the world's foremost authority on leadership, organizational development, and change management, he is also the author of three bestselling books, including *Compassionate Capitalism: A Journey to the Soul of Business* (co-authored with David Meltzer). Avatar Resources now has offices in four countries and has consulted to some of the world's biggest companies. Bartlett also enjoys teaching millennials how they can reframe any negative into a positive and use their enterprising nature to create a future of endless possibilities.

Bartlett also found happiness in his personal life again, recently marrying Cynthia, who shares his vision for compassionate capitalism.

THE BRAIN
A BROADCASTING AND RECEIVING
STATION FOR THOUGHT

~/\~

*"All impulses of thought have a
tendency to clothe themselves in
their physical equivalent."*
—Napoleon Hill

THE BRAIN IS THE CONDUIT FOR ALL SUCCESS AND failure. As a broadcasting and receiving station for thought, it acts on the vibrations that it deems most necessary for what you want in your life. Emotionally charged thoughts, whether good or bad, stimulate the brain at a higher rate of vibration and are therefore more readily transformed into massive action.

In a democracy, those who wish to enact legislative change can only do so with the majority support of their people. To achieve this, great political leaders tap into the emotionally charged frequencies communicated between their own party and the prospective voting population. President Barack Obama's "Yes We Can" slogan and President Donald Trump's "Make America Great Again" were both highly instrumental in getting them elected. Through their campaigns, both Obama and Trump clearly outlined their purpose, evoked a strong emotional response directed toward a constructive end, and aligned their frequencies with the public. In doing so, they have been able to succeed in historic political victories.

The brain, when properly calibrated to a defined outcome, uses auto-suggestion and the subconscious mind to deliver all you need to accomplish your mission. This is often achieved by latching on to similar vibrations emitted from other brains, which can be organized, paired with your own, and directed toward what you desire. In contrast, those with negative vibrations broadcast the emotions of anger, fear, and hate, and those with weak vibrations are typically burdened with procrastination and indifference.

Paradoxically, the only way to have great physical wealth in your life is to harness the necessary *intangible* forces to acquire it. Yet, rather than look within, too many people blame the world for the wealth that eludes them or lack of opportunities that come their way. Fortunately, the solution is readily available to anyone who learns how to apply the achievement philosophy. Remember, every great achievement through history was once a simple impulse of thought. The person who calibrates their brain as a powerful broadcasting station for good will find it quickly gets to work on all the necessary actions to attain that which they desire.

You have a supercomputer in your own head that, through the vibration of thought, can create an immensely powerful network and readily transmute it to physical means. Momentum swells with the countless people you recruit to your definite end. Start with your burning desire, then use your most powerful asset for it to manifest physically.

Dennis Kimbro

Startled, Dennis Kimbro looked up from his book. In 1950—the year of his birth—only five of the 100,000 millionaires in the United States were African American. The college student's life would never be the same after reading that statistic. He had always held a passion for solving inequality around the world, but now it moved closer to home—to the struggle for racial equality in the United States, his home country. Kimbro committed to speaking with the most successful African American men and women he could find so he could share their secrets in an effort to balance the wealth gap.

After completing his undergraduate studies, Kimbro listed the names of 50 of the most successful African American people he could think of and started to interview them. As he traveled the country conducting the interviews, he became aware of more and more people he could add to the list, which eventually grew to more than 150 names. To help fund his travel and research expenses, Kimbro maintained jobs in the corporate world, first in pharmaceuticals and then in consulting. During each interview he would ask the same questions in an attempt to identify patterns. His plan was to draw on the interviews to publish a book, *What Makes the Great Great*, the first book of its type targeted specifically at African Americans. Excited about the prospect of sharing this message with the world, he researched wealth and poverty in underdeveloped countries, earning a doctorate degree. Then he added two key names to the list—Earl Graves and John Johnson—figuring that having interviewed them would give him instant credibility with other luminaries he might want to meet in the future.

For months, Kimbro wrote and called Graves, who was a very well-regarded entrepreneur and media publisher, but was told on each occasion: "Mr. Graves is too busy to respond to your request." Eventually, Kimbro discovered a possible link—albeit an extremely tenuous one—a friend of a friend of a friend was a distant relative of Graves, and thus was invited to a wedding that Graves was rumored to be attending. Kimbro charged his contact with a simple request: to put a handwritten note in Graves's possession. Two weeks after the wedding, and two and a half years after his initial contact, Kimbro received a phone call inviting him to Graves's office in New York for an interview. After shaking his hand, Graves looked Kimbro in the eye and said, "Young man, I admire your persistence."

As Kimbro conducted these interviews and developed his manuscript, word of his mission started to spread. Eventually, offers began to roll in from newspapers and magazines to see if the young writer was interested in contributing articles for their publications. In 1986, one of his articles published in *Success* magazine found its way to William Clement Stone, then president of the Napoleon

Hill Foundation and one of the wealthiest people in the United States. In November of that year, Stone phoned to invite the 36-year-old to his Chicago office for a meeting.

In the meeting, Kimbro was greeted warmly by Stone and then introduced to the executive director of the Napoleon Hill Foundation, Michael Ritt, and a writer and close friend of Stone's, Robert Anderson. With the requisite small talk out of the way, the three businessmen turned their attention to the matter at hand. "Let me tell you why we called you," Stone began. "The last project Napoleon Hill was working on before he passed was a book specifically written to inspire African Americans to wealth." He placed a 100-page manuscript in front of Kimbro. "It's been sitting on my desk for 16 years. We want you to co-author it, update it however you see fit, and then we can publish it for the first time."

For the past three years, Kimbro had abandoned paid work to spend all his time completing the manuscript for his own book, *What Makes the Great Great*, and was nearing its completion. The family—now with three young kids—were struggling to make ends meet. "I can help, but I need some type of financial support," he pleaded.

"No, we're not going to give you any financial help," Stone replied firmly. "When Andrew Carnegie asked Napoleon Hill to spend 20 years of his life on a single mission, Carnegie didn't pay him. And we're not going to pay you."

Kimbro shifted uncomfortably, thinking of his wife, Patricia, who had supported him for years, and how he could make this all work.

"Hold out your hand," Stone continued, before placing a medallion in his open palm. "Whoever I've given this medallion to has never failed to reach their goals and objectives." Kimbro nodded, and agreed to write the book without compensation. After the two-hour meeting, he said farewell to Stone, Ritt, and Anderson and headed to the Chicago airport for the flight home. Kimbro combed through Hill's manuscript before the plane touched down in Atlanta, Georgia.

Patricia met him at the airport. "Did they offer you a job?" she asked.

"Not exactly," he replied. "They want me to write a book."

"Another book?" Patricia said. "Did you tell them you've already been working on a book? How many books are you going to write on this!?"

While he had given his word to Stone, another three or four years on an unpaid book project was something his family could ill afford. Plagued with indecision, Kimbro focused on finishing his other book, *What Makes the Great Great*, and Hill's final work lay dormant. Four months later, Patricia said he should at least call the Napoleon Hill Foundation and tell them what was going on. Kimbro agreed, but wanted to show them some tangible proof of progress. Fortunately, he had hundreds of hours of research from his existing work, but he wanted to make sure his writing mimicked Hill's timeless writing style. With a 90-page first draft completed, he printed it out and packaged it in an overnight FedEx envelope for Chicago. But Ritt and Anderson didn't share his enthusiasm for the manuscript and threw it in the trash.

Kimbro attempted a follow-up version—this time 120 pages—and again sent it overnight to Chicago. After they discarded this second draft, Ritt phoned and said, "Dennis, you're an excellent writer. Don't feel bad—we know what we're looking for. We want to make this easy on you, so we just want you to make one change."

Kimbro replied, "Sure, what did you have in mind?"

"Take your PhD, put it on the shelf—you won't need it for this assignment. We want you to write this book as if you're writing a letter to a friend."

Reinvigorated, Kimbro updated his work with Ritt's advice, endeavoring to capture the feeling of the subject matter. Hill had only referenced three interviews in his partial manuscript, but Kimbro was determined to have the book draw on as much data as possible.

Eventually, Kimbro made it to the office of John Johnson, widely regarded as one of the country's most successful African American entrepreneurs. The first thing he noticed was a copy of *Think and Grow Rich* sitting on his desk. Johnson looked at Kimbro and asked, "Young man, why aren't you wealthy? You've got a fancy degree and your youth. If I had the resources you had, there's no telling where I would be." He tapped the cover of *Think and Grow Rich* and continued, "Here are the keys to success. All you have to do is apply them in your own life."

Kimbro paused, trying not to think of his family's struggles. It was an extremely difficult time, and they often had cashflow issues—including having the water and electricity shut off. On more than one occasion, Kimbro had used his wife's shoulder to cry on. However, despite his family's hardships, he was determined to complete the Hill project so that his six years of research and writing would not have been in vain.

In 1989, his quest led to the office of Arthur George Gaston, founder of numerous financial companies throughout the southern part of the United States. Kimbro drove from Atlanta to Birmingham, Alabama, to meet with Gaston, with Patricia and their three daughters in the car for the ride.

Kimbro and Gaston spent the afternoon together before retreating to the businessman's office for a more structured interview. Forty-five minutes later, midway through conversation, the stress of the project and trying to support his family reached a crescendo—during one of the most important meetings of his life— and Kimbro began to sob. Gaston reached across his credenza, pulled out a tissue, handed it to his interviewer, and with a curious pity asked, "What on earth is wrong!?"

"Dr. Gaston, you don't know what I've been going through. Friends and neighbors are asking why I shouldn't just get a job. I'm writing this book, and I don't know if anyone's even going to buy a copy. People are saying I'm crazy." As Kimbro vented, Gaston sat attentive but calm as he leaned into his chair. The 39-year-old continued to pour his heart out, while Gaston struck a match, lit his pipe, and took a few drags. Kimbro sat in shame, as thin lines of smoke gently filled the office.

"Tell me when you're through," Gaston said pointedly.

"Dr. Gaston, what do you mean 'tell you when I'm through'?" Kimbro stammered.

"You're going through tough times. So what? That's part of success. Greatness takes time. The acceptable person must be tested in the furnace of adversity. Fear not. Continue moving forward. But if you are satisfied and comfortable where you are in life, then step aside for the person who isn't."

Gaston's very direct advice completely reframed the situation for Kimbro. He returned to Atlanta, with the fire of determination burning in him once more, and excitedly went to work, eventually finishing and posting his manuscript for *Think and Grow Rich: A Black Choice* to the Foundation.

The following year, Kimbro was flown up to Chicago to attend a board meeting with the Foundation. As he walked in, he noticed that everyone seated around the table held a copy of his book in front of them.

Stone stood up, walked over, and asked, "Young man, what have you learned about success and achievement?"

"Well, at the counter of success there are no bargains," Kimbro responded. "You must pay the price in advance and in full."

Stone smiled, "You have indeed learned your lesson well."

In 1991, *Think and Grow Rich: A Black Choice*—authored by Dr. Dennis Kimbro and Napoleon Hill—was released, becoming an instant bestseller around the world. Six years later, Kimbro released his second book, *What Makes the Great Great*. Since then, he has consulted to some of the largest companies in the world, including Apple, Walt Disney, and Nike, and as a business school professor shares his insights with younger generations. In 2005, the National Black MBA Association presented him with the H. Naylor Fitzhugh Award, recognizing him as one of the top professors in the nation. Kimbro's fifth book, *The Wealth Choice: Success Secrets of Black Millionaires*, was released in 2013 as the culmination of a seven-year study of 1,000 of the wealthiest African Americans. He is now regarded as one of the world's foremost authorities on leadership and success.

"Wealth, prosperity, and abundance have nothing to do with race, gender, which side of the tracks you were born on, who your parents are, or your level of education," Kimbro believes. "But it has everything to do with desire, faith, and the right mental attitude. All high achievers make choices, not excuses."

Dr. Dennis Kimbro still lives in Atlanta with Patricia and their three daughters, Kelli, Kimberli, and MacKenzie. More passionate than ever, he continues his mission to help people, especially African Americans, unearth the seeds of greatness with them.

Sandy Gallagher

On August 18, 2006, over a thousand eager minds gathered at a hotel in Vancouver, Washington, for a conference with one of the world's foremost personal development and sales experts, Bob Proctor. In the crowd was corporate lawyer Sandy Gallagher.

From as far back as she could remember, Gallagher knew where she was going: she was following her father into the world of investment law. She had been studious in high school, diligent in college, and committed to her work in the corporate world.

In 1995, after seven years at a prestigious Wall Street law firm, she was ready to move back to Washington to work with her father. The father-daughter duo would create a new division for an existing firm, growing its already strong presence throughout the Pacific Northwest. The business flourished, and they built an impressive portfolio of clients, including major banking institutions. Working closely with these clients gave Gallagher a deep insight into the day-to-day operations and challenges they faced.

Several years into their journey, when the business was booming, Gallagher's father accepted an offer to serve as chief executive officer of a major investment bank. Sandy Gallagher willingly took the reins of their corporate finance partnership. Life was good—she felt happy, financially secure, and had a stable future mapped out. But something was missing.

Then in August 2006, a friend coaxed Gallagher into attending a business management and leadership seminar in Vancouver. There were more than a hundred tables of 10 people in the room, but Bob Proctor strolled out and—with his piercing eyes and trademark voice—delivered the presentation as if he were speaking with each person one on one, a skill refined over four decades of honing his craft.

Proctor enticed the crowd: "What do you want? What do you *really* want!? Are you really satisfied with what you're doing? Is this how you want to live the rest of your life?"

Instantly captivated, Gallagher felt her brain start racing. "It was 10 minutes in, and I felt like he'd taken my head off and shaken it all around," she recalls. "Had my whole life been about following someone else's dream?"

Proctor continued: "At the end of the line, are you going to look back and say, 'What have I done?'"

Gallagher was floored. Asking herself these questions, she began to expose limitations in her life that she had buried deep down. Her mindset to that point had helped her achieve the life she had wanted for as long as she could remember—seemingly, her destiny. But this speaker, whom she'd never even heard of before, asserted there was more, so much more, if she opened her eyes to what was possible.

On the spot, using the seminar workbook, Gallagher wrote three things she wanted to achieve: first, to be in the inner circle of Proctor's company; second, to be Proctor's closest adviser; and third, to create a training program with Proctor that could be rolled out to the major corporations Gallagher knew so well. She had spent almost 20 years working with executives throughout the United States and had a feeling that a carefully planned program factoring in the human dynamic would transform the way *all* these companies did business.

The next day, Gallagher stared at her own handwriting on the notepad. Self-doubt, a familiar sentiment, started to creep in, begging her to stay in her comfort zone: *Who do you think you are? You're just a lawyer.*

But something deep inside had changed. For the next 11 months, Gallagher completed as many of Proctor's programs and coaching sessions as she could find to gain an insight into his acclaimed methods. At Delray Beach, Florida, in June 2007, during one of the quarterly consultant training days, Proctor asked Gallagher to lunch. Little did she realize the personal development guru had been conducting his own due diligence on the mysterious lawyer whose name seemed to pop up everywhere he went.

During the lunch, Gallagher presented him with a comprehensive program to deliver value to the corporate world, a step-by-step guide on how to implement it, and other ideas to transform Proctor's enterprise. Proctor asked Gallagher if she'd like to come on board officially as his business partner in the companies he'd established throughout his career. It was a step Gallagher desperately wanted to take, but she struggled to justify the career change. To that point, her whole life had been about calculation, planning, evaluating risk, and acting on logic. She was still head of the law practice and had a very clear future path plotted out. Proctor again asked what she thought about the idea.

"I wonder what my dad's going to think," she blurted out.

"How old are you?" Proctor asked. "You're still wondering what your dad's going to think!?"

Gallagher had made a success of her childhood dream, one that stemmed from admiration and respect for her father and his career. But sharing a dream with her father from such an early age, Gallagher had never questioned whether that was really what she wanted to do with her life. It had never occurred to her that her dream might not have been what her heart truly desired.

Returning to Seattle, Gallagher emailed her friends and family to advise them of her career change. Hundreds of people responded, wishing her well in her new career, but three replies from well-respected attorneys stood out—all with a similar theme. "I wish I could do something like that, but I'm going to sit here at this desk until the day I die," they read. These people, who were incredibly successful by almost every definition, felt trapped in their line of work despite their income, education, and material possessions.

It was a common thread she had observed throughout her career, first with recently graduated associates whose lives were confined to an office, then with lawyers who felt that—because they'd done something for the last 20 years—they were shackled to it forever. "They didn't know that at any time they could do whatever they wanted," Gallagher lamented.

From that day forward, she started working with Proctor. In January 2009, they created the Proctor Gallagher Institute, with Gallagher at the helm as CEO. The business was born with a single goal: to get one of their life-changing programs into every household in the country.

Shortly after founding the company, Gallagher asked Proctor, "Can you help me to teach like you?" He offered her the same affirmation that wealthy industrialist Andrew Carnegie once gave young reporter Napoleon Hill, only it was switched from the future to the past tense. Gallagher nodded, closed her eyes, and muttered: "Bob Proctor, I not only matched your achievements in life, I challenged you at the post and passed you at the grandstand."

Proctor reminded her that it would seem fantastical unless and until she believed it. She repeated it again, louder and with more resolve.

"Bob Proctor, I not only matched your achievements in life, I challenged you at the post and passed you at the grandstand."

Today, Sandy Gallagher shares the stage with her mentor at sold-out conferences throughout the world. Their company, the Proctor Gallagher Institute, has more than 800 certified consultants, programs translated into multiple languages, and hosts life-changing events for as many people as they can reach— from those at the start of their self-help journey, to aspiring entrepreneurs, right through to top-level executives.

Gallagher, the former corporate lawyer, has never been happier. "Whatever you love, that's the fuel," she offers. "Regardless of who you are, there's no box you have to fit into."

With a new lease on life, Gallagher spends her time asking people the one question that changed it all: "What do you want—what do you *really* want!?"

THE SIXTH SENSE
THE DOOR TO THE TEMPLE OF WISDOM

"All people are who they are because of
their dominating thoughts and desires."
—NAPOLEON HILL

THE SIXTH SENSE DESCRIBES THE CONDITION IN WHICH Infinite Intelligence communicates willingly and seamlessly without an individual's conscious effort. Coming in the form of a hunch or inspiration, it is received separately from the five senses and only emerges to its true capacity when the preceding principles are mastered.

The sixth sense is the apex of the achievement philosophy and the key to prolonged happiness in all areas of one's life. However, workable knowledge of this principle's power eludes most until they reach their forties or fifties and comes only after considerable self-examination, experience, and reflection.

The stories included here, and in the original *Think and Grow Rich*, reveal the extraordinary journeys of people who have been able to translate their instinctual knowledge to great advantage. It's the sixth sense that Rob Dyrdek describes as his "rhythm of existence playbook," the confidence that Grant Cardone knows will lead him to positively impact the lives of almost every person on earth, and the unwavering belief that Sandy Gallagher will surpass her mentor's achievements in life as Hill did Carnegie's.

The sixth sense foretells danger in time to avoid it, just as readily as it seeks opportunity in time to embrace it. Those in survival situations have often found themselves prompted to undertake an action that saves their lives, generally via a hard-to-describe impulse. An extreme example is that of Maurice and Maralyn Bailey, a British couple who survived 117 days on a life raft in the Pacific Ocean. Drifting at the mercy of wind and wave, the Baileys caught fish with hooks fashioned out of safety pins and experienced the urge to consume the fish eyes—a culinary treat they would not have enjoyed in their regular lives. But fish eyes contain fresh water and essential nutrients: that urge enabled them to rehydrate and consume essential vitamins that saved their lives.

Regardless of what term you use to describe it, the sixth sense is profoundly spiritual, aligning individual purpose with the universe, so that everything that comes along can be immediately directed to constructive use— it feels like everything, in fact, does happen for a reason. This principle cannot be practiced or disproved; however, those who have not experienced its power firsthand, spoken to those impacted by it, or personally studied the philosophy can be impeded by their own skepticism and doubt. They are destined to continue receiving whatever life gives them, rather than what they want.

We can only create that which we have seen as a thought impulse. Through consistent application of Hill's preceding principles, the sixth sense is gently summoned and becomes the highway that delivers inspiration to your conscious mind for action, whether in the form of new business ventures, a prospective relationship, or invention of a groundbreaking product or service. Those who attribute their ongoing prosperity to Hill's work can readily attest to its power.

As shown by the countless lives changed since *Think and Grow Rich* was first published in 1937, it is the simple but consistent practice of applying these principles that leads to self-mastery, and ultimately to prolonged success.

Don Green

"Can I have $6 for a boy scout uniform?" eight-year-old Don Green asked.

"We can't waste your daddy's money because we don't know when he may get hurt in the mines," his mom replied.

Green nodded. If he wanted money, he would need to earn it himself.

Growing up in Wise, Virginia, Green's parents were part of a generation scarred from the Great Depression—they believed that when opportunity faded, a strong work ethic was your most valuable asset. From the moment Green and his brothers could walk, they were taught the value of hard work and given odd jobs to do, from toiling in the fields to tending their neighbor's property. Anytime they complained, their mother would shout from the house, "Hard work never killed anybody!"

Green's father worked in the coalmines, earning 75 cents an hour. The coal seam stood just three feet high, so the workers would be seated or hunched over as they chipped away. He endured the back-breaking labor and hazardous conditions because it was regular pay, which allowed the Green family to put food on the table. To supplement their father's income from the coalmines, the family would sell herbs to the local market.

While hunting ginseng in the forest could be lucrative, it was inconsistent.

Green enjoyed joining his father on these trips and helping contribute to the household finances. He would take a tool, dig up the herbs, rinse the dirt off, dry the herbs, and then transport them to the local market for payment. He still says that selling mayapple for $3 was the best money he's ever earned, and adds: "If you earn it through hard work, you think twice before you spend it."

The process of working, selling, and saving became an enjoyable habit for Green. As he started high school, he explored creative ideas to make money. He began reading books and became fascinated with the stories of Abraham Lincoln, Thomas Jefferson, and George Washington. He then found an author, Napoleon Hill, who also hailed from Wise. Green became so enamored with his hometown hero that he read as much of his work as he could find, then turned to the sources that Hill himself had enjoyed—Ralph Waldo Emerson, Elbert Hubbard, and Samuel Smiles. One passage in particular got him thinking laterally: *You make wages with your hands. You make good money with your head.*

Green saw his father's daily struggles and learned through books that a lifelong commitment to education and business skills would create freedom for the rest of his life. "If it's to be, it's up to me," he told himself.

Green would use the classroom as a creative workshop to plan high-earning ventures. One year, during the two-week break for Christmas, all his school friends stayed home with their families. But the 15-year-old had drawn up a plan for a seasonal Christmas tree business—how many he could cut, what he could sell them for, and where they would best be sold. He followed through on his plan, cutting trees and selling them on the side of a busy road—earning almost $100; outstanding pay for two weeks out of school.

Green went on to college, graduating with an undergraduate degree in business and accounting. As he began his search for a white-collar job, he made a vow to his cousin that one day he would be bank president. To achieve this goal, he hunkered down—reading and studying like never before.

When he applied for a job with a finance company, Green rented a suit and borrowed his uncle's car for the interview. He was hired, but knew it would take daily effort to prove himself worthy in the new role. He worked 60 hours a week, which quickly earned him the moniker "Hot Shot" among his peers, and continually searched for opportunities to go the extra mile. Green also signed up for every training and educational program the company offered. Each fortnight he collected his pay of $110, equating to just shy of $1 an hour.

After a few years, Green applied for, and was accepted into, the Stonier Graduate School of Banking at Rutgers. At the same time, he obtained a new job in the collections department of a local bank. His schooling at Rutgers required him to complete a thesis—the topic he selected was "The Organization and Implementation of a Credit Department at a Community Bank." Green worked and researched diligently, using his experience from the finance company and knowledge of the bank from his current job, and graduated with top marks.

After eight years, the community bank received a generous offer to sell, and Green decided it was time to move on. Still determined to make it into the upper echelons of the finance industry, he applied for a job as president with another bank and was accepted. At 41 years old, Don Green had achieved his goal.

However, the new bank—like many in the state—was in financial strife, and Green had the unenviable task of turning the company's fortunes around. Given the dire circumstances, he was able to negotiate stock options that at the time were almost worthless but would offer tremendous upside if his mission was successful. His first order of business was to give the staff a pay raise. The trustees asked if he was crazy, but he persisted, responding firmly, "We'll make the money."

Drawing on his in-depth knowledge of the banking system and consumer loans, Green personally met with banking clients who had 30-year loans and demonstrated how much money they could save if they reduced the term by half. Most agreed. Not only did the bank start receiving better cashflow, but Green also strengthened relationships with its customers.

At the time, it was standard practice for banks to foreclose on people who hadn't met the interest payments on their mortgages. But Green reasoned that once you foreclosed, any ongoing relationship with the customer was eliminated. He wanted to implement appropriate systems that would also ensure the bank could transact with them in the future. Leading by example, he showed customer after customer that he cared for them and understood their difficult situation, reiterating that seizing their car or home was the last thing he wanted to do. He then offered to meet the customer wherever was most convenient for them so he could collect their overdue payment. With this two-pronged approach of maneuvering the bank's resources to enable better collections, coupled with genuine care for its customers, Green created a win-win for both parties. Throughout a 20-year career, under Green's management, the bank did not foreclose on a single home.

Green's other projects, away from the bank, were starting to build too. Since first reading of the concept at a young age, he had dreamed of earning a greater income from something outside his salaried role, so he kept an eye out for any enterprising opportunities. From all his experience in the white-collar world, Green had built quite a suit collection, with more than 30 sitting in his wardrobe. Alas, they needed to be cleaned regularly, but he'd had very mixed results using the existing dry cleaning businesses in town. One day, he noticed a DIY dry cleaning kit advertised in a magazine and ordered it for $39.99.

When the kit arrived, he studied every step to identify why a seemingly simple task was often mishandled.

He approached some friends and asked, "If I build a dry cleaner, would you use it?" They agreed unanimously. Green got plans drawn up and built a dry cleaning business on a piece of land he owned near the bank.

The dry cleaning business opened with higher prices than its competitors, but Green refused to advertise, preferring to let word of mouth drive their sales. He insisted that the quality of its work should speak loudest. The new business introduced same-day service—a dramatic shift from the standard one-week turnaround—which had never been done in that region. People would drop their clothes off on the way to work and pick them up later that day on their way home. Green's business also offered a drive-through service so that people could do what they needed without ever leaving their car. The business boomed from day one, which made Green happy—but having his suits cleaned just the way he liked brought the biggest smile to his face.

Another of his goals was to buy 100 stocks in 10 companies. When dividends were paid, he would automatically have them reinvested. When he had enough extra money in his account, he would buy more shares. Soon, he had reached 1,000 shares of 10 different companies. As the portfolio grew, he was not just receiving dividend payments but growth from the stock, too.

He was also heavily invested in the ongoing development of his staff. At the bank he created and taught a workshop, which he called "Keys to Success," based on the principles outlined in Hill's work. The most important part of the curriculum was not memorizing facts that could be regurgitated later, but demonstrating practical understanding of the principles and applying them to real-world scenarios.

Several years later, retail conglomerate Walmart was eyeing a territory to open its new store, and Green heard a whisper it might be on the land his dry cleaning business was on. Sure enough, a Walmart agent stopped by to ask if he was interested in selling the property. "Two million dollars," he responded.

"The land ain't worth that!" the agent replied.

"We're making money. Do you want to look at my books? Not a penny less than $2 million."

Three days later, they came back with a cashier's check, without even asking to look at his books. Green sold the dry cleaning equipment to a friend who wanted to start one of his own and left the cleaning industry. Several years later, at 60 years old, Green left the bank and sold his stock—his hard work to turn the bank around had been handsomely rewarded.

But Green wasn't ready to retire; his work ethic was still strong. He wrote to the Napoleon Hill Foundation, based in Chicago, to let them know about the educational programs he had been running at the bank. The

Foundation responded, inviting him to Chicago to meet with the board. Shortly after, they asked if he would be interested in running the Foundation. Green agreed, on the condition that they bring the Foundation's headquarters back to Wise, where Hill was born and Green resided.

Today, Don Green has served as executive director of the Napoleon Hill Foundation for 17 years. Under his guidance, the Foundation—with its motto "Make the world a better place to live"—has more than 300 publishers around the world and has funded hundreds of college scholarships. Despite his long list of accolades, Green rates his favorite accomplishment as his 54-year marriage to his wife, Phyllis.

Green has also been instrumental in making self-help material accessible in all corners of the globe, in every rung of society—from schools to prisons and everywhere in between. It's his hope that with the right guidance and education, people from all walks of life can realize their infinite potential.

CONCLUSION

EVERYTHING YOU NEED TO CREATE A TRULY RICH life is already in your possession. Hopefully, at this juncture, you feel a burning desire for something you wish to achieve and have prepared a detailed plan on how to get it. If not, start immediately, before that inspiration gives way to comfort and familiarity. Follow the achievement philosophy outlined here (and in the 1937 *Think and Grow Rich*), and everything else you need will be found along the way.

When you change your thoughts, you change the world in which you live. For enduring success and self-mastery, you must not only study each of the principles until you truly understand them, but also consistently apply daily action with your end goal in mind. Use emotionally-charged repetitive thought, put your definite purpose in writing, and repeat it aloud each day in a state of enthusiasm. Through this action, the subconscious mind will get to work on finding everything you need on your journey, eliminating distractions, and translating simple ideas to massive results over time.

To emerge victorious in your mission, have faith in its eventual attainment, persist when adversity strikes, and surround yourself with those who can help make it happen. Willingly eradicate bad habits, and instill positive, productive behaviors in their place. When you come across a bump in the road, recalibrate your plans and advance once more. If this seems too arduous, remind yourself that those who are unwilling to pay the price for their success must cede their dreams to those who will.

The stories in this book remind us of the enormous potential just waiting to be ignited inside all of us, regardless of how dire our circumstances may appear. Remember—your dream will only work if you do. Consistently and excitedly apply the same achievement philosophy that has catapulted everyday people to extraordinary success for 80 years.

Live a life of purpose and fulfillment—for you and those around you. That is your mission, and that is the legacy of *Think and Grow Rich*.

ABOUT THE AUTHOR

JAMES WHITTAKER
B.Bus(Mgt), AdvDipFS(FP), MBA

James Whittaker has more than 15 years of experience with both corporate and startup companies in Australia and the United States. In 2010, he co-authored the bestselling personal finance and motivation book *The Beginner's Guide to Wealth*. He has interviewed more than 100 of the world's most revered entrepreneurs, business icons, and athletes to unlock their secrets to success. Today, in addition to being the co-executive producer of the 2017 film *Think and Grow Rich: The Legacy*, James is the co-founder/director of several companies in the health and fitness industry. His mission is to share the success habits of high performers to give younger generations the tools to take ownership of their financial, physical, and mental health.

James can be contacted via his website, jameswhitt.com, or via email at james@jameswhitt.com.

ACKNOWLEDGMENTS

To prepare a book that would do justice to Napoleon Hill's enormous legacy required the unwavering support of many. First, to the extremely hard-working and passionate team that put the wheels in motion to bring the *Think and Grow Rich: The Legacy* project to life, in particular to Sean Donovan, Karina Donovan, Joel Franco, and film director Scott Cervine. Thank you for bringing me into the fold, trusting my creative vision, and providing a platform for us to change the world.

The stories included within this book would not be possible without the entrepreneurs, cultural icons, and thought leaders who courageously rose above their circumstances to create a truly remarkable life. Thank you for not only giving up valuable time in your immensely busy schedules, but for so willingly and candidly sharing your inspirational stories with me. In particular, to Bob Proctor for your lifelong passion for *Think and Grow Rich*—I can think of no one better to have written the foreword.

To David Wildasin and the Sound Wisdom publishing team for understanding the vision and helping us bring it to life. Your unconditional support, creative guidance, and belief in the project has been truly invaluable. A special thank you also to Helena Bond for making herself available at all hours of the day and night to help shape, refine and edit the entire contents of this book. To Noel and Gerri for leading a life of steadfast integrity, and Jenn for her patience, support, and understanding of the personal sacrifices required.

Of course, to Napoleon Hill—a young reporter of humble beginnings—who held a selfless vision for global prosperity. It has been the greatest honor of my life to learn more about your extraordinary journey; we will work diligently to ensure your legacy lives on forever. Thank you to Don Green and the Napoleon Hill Foundation for continuing to offer materials that allow people to change their lives, and your unconditional support in helping us reintroduce the timeless classic to the world.

Finally, to everyone who reads this book and takes consistent, purposeful action. Everything you need to succeed is already within your possession—just follow the proven blueprint of those who have gone before you.